TELL ME, JESUS, WHO YOU ARE

For
Sarah and Joe Mooren
and
Molly and Greg Mooren

John F. Craghan

Tell Me, Jesus, Who You Are

Re-discovering Jesus
in the Sunday Gospels

DOMINICAN PUBLICATIONS

First published (2018) by
Dominican Publications
42 Parnell Square
Dublin 1

ISBN 978-1-905604-36-4

British Library Cataloguing in Publications Data.
A catalogue record for this book is available
from the British Library.

Copyright © (2018) The Author and Dominican Publications

All rights reserved.
No part of this publication may be reproduced, stored in
a retrieval system or transmitted by any means,
electronic or mechanical, including photocopying,
without permission in writing from the publisher.

Acknowledgement
Scripture texts in this work are taken from the *New American Bible*,
revised edition © 2010, 1991, 1986, 1970 Confraternity of Christian
Doctrine, Washington, D.C. and are used by permission of the
copyright owner. All Rights Reserved. No part of the *New American
Bible* may be reproduced in any form without permission in writing
from the copyright owner.

Cover design by David Cooke

Cover Image
Statue of Jesus Christ surrounded by Four Evangelists and angels
above the entrance to the Cathedral of Chartres (France).

Printed in Ireland by
Digital Print Dynamics
Ballycoolin, Dublin 11

Contents

Preface — 7

1 The Gospel of Mark — 9

Prologue: The Beginning of the Good News
The Authority and Power of Jersus in Word and Deed
Jesus' Activity around the Sea of Galilee
Journey to Jerusalem
The Ministry of Jesus in Jerusalem
Eschatological Discourse
Jesus' Suffering, Death and Resurrection
Concluding Reflections on the Jesus of Mark

2 The Gospel of Matthew — 33

Jesus' Origins
Beginning of Jesus' Ministry
Speech 1: The Sermon on the Mount
Jesus' Mighty Deeds
Speech 2: The Missionary Discourse
The Rejection of Jesus
Speech 3: The Parables of the Kingdom
Miracles, Controversies and the Cross
Speech 4: Advice to a Divided Community
Opposition to Jesus
Speech 5: The Eschatological Discourse
The Passion, Death and Resurrection of Jesus
Concluding Reflections on the Jesus of Matthew

3 The Gospel of Luke   65

   Prologue
   Infancy
   Preparation for Jesus' Public Ministry
   Jesus' Galilean Ministry
   Jesus Journeys to Jerusalem
   The Ministry of Jesus in Jerusalem
   The Passion Narrative
   Resurrection Narratives
   Concluding Reflections on the Jesus of Luke

4 The Gospel of John   103

   Prologue
   The Book of Signs
   The Book of Glory and First Conclusion of the Gospel
   Epilogue
   Concluding Reflections on the Gospel of John

   Liturgical Index   129

Preface

Since 1969 the Church has benefited from the new lectionary for Sundays with its three-year cycle of readings. As a result, the faithful now get to hear the distinctive voices of Matthew ('A' cycle), Mark ('B' cycle), Luke ('C' cycle), and John (principally Lenten and Easter seasons). With this significant change the liturgy has caught up to the progress in biblical studies that have emphasized the particular posture and focus of each evangelist.

At the same time, however, the faithful appear to need more than the comments of the homilist to appreciate the distinctive portrait of Jesus in each evangelist. Instead of following the chronological order of the readings, this guide seeks to develop this portrait according to the order of the biblical text itself. The Liturgical Index will enable a homilist seeking a commentary for a particular Sunday or festival to find it in these pages.

This work appreciates the dilemma of worshippers who seek to recover the identity of Jesus of Nazareth in the course of the three-year cycle. To be sure, they would like to possess photos of Jesus, recordings of his key sermons, and more factual information about the details of his infancy, youth, and ministry. Although these items are totally lacking, believers still possess in the gospels a treasure trove of incidents, sayings, and controversies involving Jesus. In the end they must trust the evangelists and realize that, though they will not provide the biographical data they would like, nonetheless the evangelists can enable them to rediscover the richness of the person of Jesus.

To begin with, believers must recognize Matthew, Mark, Luke, and John as real writers who have provided distinctive interpretations of Jesus. In a word, they are authors. Unlike modern fiction writers, they do not create their stories from their own imagination. Rather, they have access to both oral and written traditions about Jesus. However, they do not compress them into a dry anthology. Instead, they create gospels, namely, the good news about Jesus and the significance of his life, death, and resurrection. As the Dogmatic Constitution on Divine Revelation of Vatican II states, the gospels must be read at three distinct but related levels: Jesus, the early church, and the evangelists themselves. As such, the evangelists put modern believers in touch not only with Jesus but also with the development of Christian communities and their own concerns. In this last area the evangelists shape their message about Jesus to address the specific needs of their communities. Modern believers thus form part of that long line that begins in Palestine and impinges on today's world.

Unfortunately we know relatively little about Matthew, Mark, Luke, and John. The titles at the beginning of their works ('The Gospel according to…') appear to go back only to the second century and may not rest on solid historical traditions. Although anonymous, the evangelists continue to challenge ever new generations of believers. They focus on perennial issues that confront all followers of Jesus, *e.g.*, the meaning of faith, the demands of community life, and the need to live out the gospel message in the fray of daily existence. It is not surprising, therefore, that the gospels enjoy pride of place in the order of readings at Sunday liturgy. (The gospels of the Sacred Triduum [Holy Thursday, Good Friday, and Holy Saturday] are included in this work since they are central to the work of the evangelists. The gospels of the holy days of obligation are included as well.)

I dedicate this work to Sarah and Joe Mooren as well as Molly and Greg Mooren who regularly attend the 7:00 A.M. Sunday Mass with me along with their families at Holy Spirit Church in Darboy, WI. The presence of both parents and children at this Sunday liturgy challenges me to elaborate the identity of Jesus that they will share as families and members of our worshipping community. In this way the gospel portrait of each evangelist extends beyond the confines of our worship space to embrace the rough-and-tumble of everyday life.

Finally, I thank my wife, Barbara Lynne Wenzel Craghan, for her helpful suggestions and observations in critiquing the manuscript. She thereby helps me to rediscover the identity of Jesus in yet another form.

The Jesus of Mark

The Setting of the Gospel of Mark

Since the author of this gospel has not provided any firm date or clear background for his composition, the interpreter is compelled to look for clues that may suggest some probable answers. From an overall reading of the text one encounters a community that has endured persecution from without and division from within. Right from the opening chapter the Cross casts its unmistakable shadow over the entire work. For example, John the Baptist preaches and is handed over or arrested. Thereafter, Jesus and subsequent believers experience the same fate.

The theme of division among Jesus' disciples also plays a prominent role in the work. In addition, persecutions figure significantly in the gospel. When one puts all these observations together, there surface images of an early Christian community that has endured pain for the name of Jesus and most likely was anticipating more suffering.

A likely setting for the writing of the gospel is the persecution of Christians under Nero because of the great fire of 64 A.D. In order to shift blame from himself for the fire, Nero attributed the conflagration to Roman Christians. The Roman historian Tacitus relates that Nero had Christians arrested and then convicted. He also imposed harsh punishments on those convicted. To make matters worse, Christians betrayed fellow Christians. Apostasy was rife indeed.

The author of Mark probably writes his gospel around the year 70 A.D. (This was also the year in which the Romans utterly destroyed the Jewish temple in Jerusalem.) He clearly demonstrates that Christian discipleship and suffering go hand in hand. To accept the message of Jesus is to embrace the cross. The Jesus of Mark is undeniably the suffering Messiah. As Jesus unequivocally states in 8:31, 'the Son of Man must suffer greatly and be rejected by the elders, the chief priests, and the scribes, and be killed, and rise after three days.' Ironically, the infidelity of the disciples in this gospel, notably Peter, becomes good news for those who experience failure, especially apostasy. Like Peter, they are called to repentance and reconciliation. The Cross points to the empty tomb.

Prologue: The Beginning of the Good News (1:1-13)

John the Baptist Announces the Coming One (1:1-8)

This passage marks the beginning of Mark's message for his distraught community. The story of Jesus can now unfold with the proclamation of John the Baptist. The audience is to learn that neither the formidable power of evil nor the crushing brutality of the powers-that-be will enjoy the last word.

The Baptist senses God's presence in the person of Jesus. He also understands his own mission in terms of precursor – he is to prepare the way of the Lord. Specifically, he prepares the people for the arrival of 'one mightier' than he by his proclamation of radical conversion. He proceeds to demonstrate the seriousness of his intent by appearing in the guise of Elijah (camel's hair clothing and leather belt). He emphasizes the centrality of Jesus by seeing himself only in the role of a herald. Jesus, not he, is to occupy centre stage.

John Baptises Jesus (1:7-11)

In recounting the baptism of Jesus by John, Mark underlines Jesus' vision and the heavenly voice. The tearing open of the heavens recalls Isaiah 63:19 where the prophet begs God to rend the heavens and come down. The second element in Jesus' vision is the descent of the dove-like Spirit. The role of the Spirit in Jesus' ministry is paramount for Mark since it will enable him to carry out his mission. The heavenly voice establishes a unique form of communication between God and Jesus. Mark thereby identifies Jesus as both God's Son and his beloved servant (see Isaiah 42:1-2).

For Mark's audience this scene is good news indeed since it reveals that God has not forgotten them. Rather, through Jesus he has established a special form of communication. The result is that heaven and earth are now in contact. As Son, Jesus enjoys a special bond with God, a bond that he will manifest in his moments of prayer. As beloved Son, Jesus is also the Suffering Servant who will achieve his mission by coping with pain on behalf of his people. As no stranger to suffering, Jesus easily appeals to Mark's audience. He will, however, ultimately triumph but only at the cost of his life. As God's servant, Jesus can empathize with the experience of Mark's audience. The shadow of the Cross is painfully present.

Jesus is Tempted in the Desert (1:12-15)

The author Mark clearly links Jesus' temptation in the desert with the baptism. There, Jesus experiences the divine world in the communication from the Father. In the temptation, however, he is in the desert or wilderness, *i.e.*, the demonic world, the traditional haunt of the evil forces. 'Forty days' suggests a link with the 40 years of Israel's wandering in the desert or wilderness. Whereas Israel failed during that period, here Jesus succeeds. The author also seems to imply a certain messianic element in this scene, namely, the type of messiahship Jesus would embrace. Jesus thus begins his battle with Satan and the powers of evil. His death and subsequent resurrection will resolve the form of his messiahship and his relationship to the powers of evil.

In the conclusion of this passage the author begins the account of the public ministry of Jesus with a summary. He notes the fate of the Baptist and suggests that the Cross cannot be divorced from a consideration of the person and mission of Jesus. In Jesus, God's kingdom, *i.e.*, his providing for the needs of his people, has finally dawned. In Jesus, the new age has begun. The audience is thus invited to adopt a new way of thinking that will lead to a new way of acting ('repentance') and put their trust in the good news of salvation that comes in the person of Jesus.

Mark thus presents a Jesus bound up with the world of chaos. Satan and the powers of evil personify that chaos, one that brings in its wake human sickness, perversion, and isolation. The task of Jesus is to overcome such chaotic forces. The struggle in the desert or wilderness is the beginning of Jesus' containing of chaos. He proceeds to offset such chaos by proclaiming hope in the form of the kingdom of God, God's definitive intervention in which he will provide for all the needs of his people. The person of Jesus is God's finest expression of hope for a chaotic world.

The Authority and Power of Jesus in Word and Deed (1:14 — 3:6)

Jesus Calls His First Four Disciples (1:14-20)

The first two verses of this passage repeat the summary of Jesus' public ministry given above. Today's passage, however, forges a link between the ministry of Jesus and that of his disciples. In other words, Jesus rejects working alone. Instead, he reaches out for collaborators who will continue his ministry. Jesus is clearly a team player.

In this call of the first disciples Mark presents Jesus' invitation and the disciples' response. To follow Jesus demands total dedication and radical renunciation. The first pair of brothers (Simon and Andrew) illustrates this total dedication while the second pair (James and John, the sons of Zebedee) highlights the radical renunciation (see 1 Kings 19:19-21). The disciples of Jesus differ from those of the rabbis. The latter seek out the rabbi while Jesus seeks out and invites the former. The person of Jesus is the core reality of discipleship for Mark.

To summarize, the call of the first four disciples embraces six elements. First, Jesus takes the initiative. Second, those called are engaged in ordinary kinds of work. Third, the call is a clear summons (v 17: 'Come after me'). Fourth, the call is to participate in the ministry of the One calling. Fifth, the response to the call brooks no hesitation or reflection and results in the abandonment of one's former occupation. Sixth, the response to the call is communal in that one chooses membership in a group.

Jesus Cures a Man with an Unclean Spirit (1:21-28)

Together with the healing of Peter's mother-in-law (1:29-31) and the healings at evening (1:32-34), this episode, consisting of teaching and exorcism, is intended to provide a picture of a typical day in Jesus' early ministry. Mark develops Jesus' divine authority and invites the reader to observe the crowd's reaction. The crowd is astonished – it does not yet perceive the full import of the action of God's Son.

Mark shows Jesus teaching in the synagogue where he probably delivers the homily. However, his manner of teaching is decidedly different from that of the lay experts, the scribes. Jesus does not cite the various rabbis. His manner is prophetic. It is new teaching backed up with his own authority.

An 'unclean spirit' implies illness, often mental illness which was thought to be due to demonic influence. Jesus' exorcism is nothing less than a frontal attack on the realm of the demons. Jesus appears as one who cannot tolerate anything that oppresses and depresses the human spirit. The unclean spirit acknowledges such a frontal attack by asking: 'Have you come to destroy us?' (v 24) The demon also seeks to overpower Jesus by recognizing him as 'the Holy One of God.' (No human recognizes Jesus' special relationship to God until the centurion does so in 15:39.) The unclean spirit, therefore, is more perceptive than the crowd. Eschewing the more elaborate rites of contemporary exorcists, Jesus simply issues a command and the unclean spirit obeys. In Mark's presentation Jesus has now begun to disclose his real self.

At Simon's House Jesus Carries out Many Healings (1:29-39)

In Mark's ongoing picture of Jesus' typical day both exorcisms and healings witness the impact of the arrival of the kingdom and therefore salvation. For Mark's audience, Peter's mother-in-law symbolizes the disciple whom the Lord has raised up (v 31: 'helped her up') and who is then commissioned to serve (v 31: 'she waited on them').

As this passage continues, there are more healings and exorcisms. ' ... because they knew him' (34) implies the demons' awareness of who Jesus really is and his unwillingness to disclose his true identity. (Mark puts off revealing Jesus' true identity until his death and resurrection [see 9:9]). At the close of this passage Mark depicts the disciples as popularity seekers who are upset because Jesus loses a great chance to display his powers. Jesus corrects the misconception by indicating that his purpose is not to satisfy the curiosity of the Capernaum crowds but to carry out the mission of his Father. The concluding verse illustrates this mission. He must move elsewhere so that others may benefit.

For Mark, Jesus must be a person in constant communication with God. Hence he shows Jesus retreating to a deserted place for the purpose of prayer. It is such moments of prayer that energize Jesus in the execution of his mission. Without prayer Jesus will not be able to do God's will.

Jesus Cleanses a Leper (1:40-45)

The cleansing of the leper is a significant scene here in the beginning of Mark's Gospel. Leprosy, that was not limited to Hansen's disease but included a wide variety of skin problems, separated the victim from family and community. In this episode Mark shows that the kingdom is accessible to all and that its very notion means the overthrow of everything that impedes genuine community relations. Where the Jewish community could only erect barriers against this affliction, *e.g.*, not touching a leper, Jesus is ready to tear them down by re-admitting the leper to community. The conclusion: namely, Jesus' growing popularity, reveals the people's acceptance of Jesus' intent.

In cleansing the leper, Jesus encounters another form of evil that he must overcome in establishing the kingdom. Given the defensive measures against leprosy, it is telling that Jesus actually touches the leper and thereby violates Jewish ritual law. What is perhaps even more significant is Jesus' motive in this scene. He is moved to compassion, an emotion that reveals Jesus' shared humanity with the victim. In bridging the gap between the holy and the unclean, Jesus comes across as one whose mission is to make humanity whole again.

The reaction of the cured man is to proclaim the good news. Here Mark's audience is invited to see itself. They too have been cleansed in Baptism and have thereby assumed the obligation to announce the good news about Jesus. In their daily proclamation of such good news the miracle of the cleansing lives on.

Jesus Heals a Paralytic (2:1-12)

This episode is part of a larger complex of conflict stories (2:1–3:6). This complex explains in part the hostility towards Jesus that culminated in his death. However, each segment in the complex is not only a debate with enemies but also a pronouncement story, *i.e.*, one that focuses on a saying or declaration by Jesus (here Jesus' power to forgive sins in verse 10). This account of the healing of the paralytic consists of two different components: (1) a miracle story (vv 1-5a,11-12) and (2) a conflict story (vv 5b-10) on the forgiveness of sins that emphasizes Jesus' pronouncement (v 10). The miracle story underlines the faith of the four litter-bearers. Here faith reveals the tenacity of suffering people to break through physical and social limitations in order to approach Jesus.

Forgiveness of sins appears to be a burning issue in Mark's community since God is believed to be the sole agent of forgiveness. Hence Jesus' opponents in this episode consider Jesus' statement about his power to forgive sins nothing short of blasphemy. Mark, however, points out that the believing community shares in the exaltation of the Son of Man and is consequently empowered to forgive sins. He is implicitly urging his community to deepen its faith by seeing the link between the exalted Son of Man and his earthly sisters and brothers. As the agent of divine forgiveness, Jesus shares this power with the community.

Jesus Discusses Fasting (2:18-22)

This passage is the third conflict story in the complex of 2:1–3:6 that consists of a conflict story about fasting (vv 18-20) and two parabolic sayings (vv 21-22). The conflict story shows that the messianic age (the bridegroom) has arrived with Jesus. Originally, the story may have dealt with the differences between the disciples of John the Baptist and the disciples of Jesus; but it may have been expanded to include the Pharisees because of the complex of conflict stories. Since only the Lord, not the Messiah, functioned as the bridegroom in the Old Testament, Mark may be implying that Jesus is on a par with the Lord. However, he will suffer death (v 20: 'taken away from them'), an event that will legitimate the practice of fasting, Until that time joy, not sorrow, is the proper response.

The two parabolic sayings clearly show that the radically new message of Jesus demands a radically new container. This new message is not a piece of cloth added to an older piece or a mixture poured into the old. The person of Jesus means that the kingdom of Jesus is a radically new event rendering the old obsolete.

Jesus Interprets Keeping Holy the Sabbath (2:23–3:6)

This passage contains the two last conflict stories in 2:1–3:6. They are: (1) the disciples and the Sabbath and (2) the man with the withered hand. The first story focuses on Jesus' freedom with regard to the Jewish law. Here Jesus enjoys the same freedom that the Old Testament grants David (see 1 Samuel 21:2-7). Sabbath observance must respect human needs. The attached sayings (vv 27-28) demonstrate that the institution is for the people, not vice versa. As a day of freedom, Sabbath means freedom not only from every kind of work but also for certain kinds of work. Jesus, therefore, as Lord of the Sabbath, liberates the Sabbath from the limitations imposed on it by non-liberated humans.

The story of the man with the withered hand looks to the concern of the Christian community in its celebration of the Lord's Day rather than the Jewish Sabbath. Jesus' statement (v 4) elaborates priorities for that celebration: good over evil, life over death. For Jesus, the real question is: How much good can one do on the Sabbath? It is not: How much good can one refrain from doing? Mark goes on to show Jesus' typically human reaction to Pharisaic blindness. His anger expresses his displeasure with the warped human values of his opponents. The indignation of the Pharisees is such that they align themselves with the supporters of Roman rule (the Herodians)—odd bedfellows indeed! This conclusion reveals the increasing hostility to Jesus that will ultimately culminate in his death.

Religious people are not infrequently tempted to identify their very human world with God's world and thereby assert their control of the holy. Here Jesus reacts to this temptation by asserting that religion must serve the needs of human beings and, therefore, human beings must never become slaves of religion. In effect, Jesus strenuously maintains that religion must foster human freedom. Any deviation from this principle is unworthy of both God and his creatures.

Jesus' Activity around the Sea of Galilee
(3:7 — 8:26)

Jesus Explains the Meaning of Discipleship (3:20-35)

This passage consists of three originally separate units that Mark has forged into a whole. It is also an example of Mark's 'sandwiching' technique in which Mark begins a narrative, then interrupts it, and finally resumes the narrative. In this instance Mark begins the account of Jesus' physical family (vv 20-21), interrupts it with the accusation of Jesus' league with Satan (vv 22-30), and then resumes the family account by speaking of Jesus' family of disciples (vv 31-35). This procedure contrasts the physical family with the family of believers.

In the opening family narrative Jesus' relatives believe he is mentally unbalanced, a state often associated with possession by the devil. In interrupting this initial narrative, Mark introduces the Jerusalem scribes who make two accusations against Jesus: (1) he is possessed by an evil spirit (v 22: 'Beelzebul') and (2) he effects his exorcisms by the power of Satan (v 22: 'the prince of demons'). Jesus replies to these accusations by means of parables. Thus a divided kingdom/household implies civil war. However, Jesus' works are clearly a frontal attack on the power of Satan – hence no evidence of civil strife. Jesus then introduces a second parable in which Satan is the mighty one but Jesus the mightier one (1:7). Owing to his exorcisms Jesus has actually overpowered Satan. Jesus' mention of blasphemy against the Holy Spirit functions as his response to the Beelzebul accusation. Whatever may have been the origin of this unforgivable sin saying, here it indicates that by attributing the exorcisms to the power of Satan one actually puts oneself outside God's kingdom. Basically, it is the refusal to acknowledge Jesus and the Spirit at work in him.

In the end Mark returns to the family narrative. Jesus' true family consists of those who do God's will. Thus those disciples gathered around Jesus are really his true relatives. Obedience to God takes precedence over kinship. Mark will focus on doing God's will during Jesus' prayer in Gethsemane (14:32-42) where he embraces his Father's will in preference to his own. To be a family member as disciple is to accept God's will while praying that things might be different.

Jesus Speaks in Parables (4:26-34)

The two parables ('seed parables') in this passage form part of Mark's sermon in parables (4:1-34). In the parable of the seed growing of itself (unique to Mark) Jesus contrasts the relative inactivity of the farmer and the certainty of the harvest. This growth cannot be thwarted in any way. Only at harvest time does the farmer reappear, a time that symbolizes the last judgment (see Revelation 14:14-20). It is likely that this parable serves as an answer to those discouraged over the progress of God's kingdom as preached by Jesus.

The parable of the mustard seed is fundamentally an appeal for patience in light of the relatively small beginnings of the kingdom. While the parable initially emphasizes the smallness of the venture, it immediately underlines the incontestable growth. God can realize such growth even though the first stages are rather inconspicuous. Jesus is thus proclaiming that the kingdom will eventually reach such proportions. In the meantime, however, patience is required.

In the final two verses Mark offers his view of Jesus' parables. He employs parables only when addressing the crowds. However, when alone with his disciples, he provides a special explanation. For Mark, therefore, the parables are by their very nature obscure so that their proper understanding demands a special revelation.

This passage contrasts Jesus' view of the kingdom with human laws of growth. The kingdom is like the seed growing of itself. Consequently humans must allow God a free hand. The kingdom is like a mustard seed. Here humans must make room for God's law of evolution. In both instances, humans are called upon to put aside purely human assessments and accept a theology of divine gift-giving.

Jesus Calms a Storm at Sea (4:35-41)

This passage initiates a series of Jesus' mighty works as he moves beyond Galilee across the lake to Gentile territory. It is the first of seven sea passages in which Jesus crosses the Sea of Galilee that symbolizes the wall of separation between Gentile and Jew. From 4:35 to 8:26 there is virtually no opposition from such nemeses as the scribes and the Pharisees. As a whole, this section portrays Jesus as the bearer of God's power in addressing human pain and suffering.

This passage is basically a miracle story that Mark had adopted for his theological purposes. The scene may be divided as follows: (1) the setting (vv 35-36); (2) the contrast between the storm and Jesus' peaceful sleep (vv 37-38a); (3) the disciples' fear and the Teacher's authoritative word (vv 38b-39); (4) Jesus' statement about lack of faith (v 40); and (5) the disciples' awe at Jesus' mighty work (v 41).

As a miracle story, this episode assumes the Old Testament understanding of the sea as a force hostile to God and humans, but one that God can nevertheless control (see Psalm 107:23-32; Isaiah 51:9-10). The disciples, therefore, experience great awe since Jesus is thus performing God's work.

Jesus chides the disciples for their timidity and lack of faith. Thus the disciples are still on a journey to true faith. Their closeness to Jesus does not absolve them from the need to enter ever more deeply into the mystery and paradox of God's kingdom.

Mark also relates this episode to the needs of his post-resurrectional community. Sensing the absence of the risen Lord, they are tempted to lose confidence in the daily struggle of Christian life. The Teacher appears to be sleeping and thus removed from their world of concern. This story assures them that lack of faith is not the proper response but that ongoing faith in the Lord at all times and in all situations alone suffices. Hence Jesus is not really asleep.

Jesus Heals the Haemorrhaging Woman and Restores Jairus' Daughter to Life (5:21-43)

In this passage Mark illustrates once again his 'sandwiching' technique. He begins with the story of the daughter of Jairus, interrupts it with the account of the haemorrhaging woman, and then resumes the initial narrative. Here Mark's purpose is to let the faith of the hemorrhaging woman have an impact on Jairus. In this way the faith of the hemorrhaging woman is to serve as a model for Jairus who has just received word of his daughter's death.

Both stories focus on life-threatening situations. In both the women are called 'daughter' and are seeking relief from their desperate conditions. In both Jesus becomes an object of ridicule as first the disciples belittle him for not seeing the crowd as the agent of touch and then the mockers at Jairus' home put him down for his comment about the young woman sleeping. Both stories also highlight the number 12: the hemorrhaging woman for the duration of her affliction and Jairus' daughter for her age.

Mark reveals Jesus' compassion for the problems of both women. The hemorrhaging woman with the problem of vaginal bleeding will be unable to bear children and, therefore, must remain unfulfilled as a woman in that society. Jairus' daughter is close to the age of marriage. However, her death will necessarily preclude any and all hope of children.

It is significant that Jesus allows the hemorrhaging woman to touch him and thereby he becomes ritually unclean. Breaking this cultic barrier, Jesus responds to her expression of faith by speaking to her in public and healing her. In the case of Jairus' daughter Jesus violates the cultural code by contracting corpse impurity. Jesus, however, sees restoration to life for a distraught father as the greater good. Jesus refuses to let illness and even death impede the good news of the kingdom.

Jesus Is Rejected at Nazareth (6:1-6)

Here Mark offers a startling contrast. In 4:35–5:43 he demonstrates Jesus' power and his acceptance. Now the opposite proves to be true. The people from his hometown reject him. (Nazareth was a small village with a meager population of several hundred in southern Galilee.) This rejection nonetheless recalls the rejection by the religious authorities in 3:6 and his family in 3:21 and foreshadows his final rejection. According to Jesus' audience here there is a glaring disproportion between his human credentials and the recent fame arising from his teaching and mighty works. After all, this audience knows his family background and his trade. He is only a carpenter or craftsman like most of the people of his day. Jesus' reaction is telling. Whereas he previously exhibited anger in connection with the religious authorities (3:4), here he shows amazement at the townspeople's lack of faith. Such a lack impedes his ability to perform any mighty deed since his use of divine power appears to depend on human response.

For Mark's audience this episode helps to explain Israel's rejection of the good news at a time when the Gentiles were accepting it. Israel is expecting another type of Messiah and Jesus does not measure up to it. Given Israel's history, this treatment of Jesus is hardly surprising. The Old Testament prophets regularly experienced such rejection. The basic issue, therefore, is the difficulty of accepting the word of a spokesperson without credentials as the word of God.

Jesus Sends the Twelve on Mission (6:7-13)

In 3:13-19 Mark relates Jesus' institution of the Twelve, his inner circle within the group of disciples. The Twelve have a symbolic role. Jesus comes as a prophet to renew Israel that derives from the twelve sons of Jacob/Israel. Since it is a question of sons, there are no women in this core group, although Jesus did have women disciples. According to 3:14-15 the Twelve have the following functions: (1) they are to be with Jesus and hence constitute a family; (2) they are to be sent out to preach; and (3) they have authority over demons.

In today's passage Jesus sends the Twelve on mission. This mission charge envisions future missionary work outside of Palestine that is construed as an extension of Jesus' own mission. Following upon Jesus' rejection in Nazareth, this episode realistically speaks of rejection. There is also a clear note of urgency in this charge. The Twelve are to rely on God for their needs. A missionary who provides for every possible emergency can hardly preach the nearness of the kingdom. Hence they are not to seek the best accommodations. Their sole proclamation is total conversion, a complete and radical reorientation (repentance). Their expulsion of demons continues Jesus' victory over Satan - hence Jesus' mission lives on in them. With a note of realism Mark mentions the act to be followed when they are rejected, namely, shaking off the dust from their feet, the removal of the last vestige of contact with a heathen environment.

In linking the ministries of Jesus, his historical disciples, and his own community, Mark insists that the Christian community is basically a missionary endeavor. As missionaries, disciples must confront the power of evil and serve as agents of God's healing power.

After the Return of the Twelve
Jesus Feeds the Five Thousand (6:30-34)

This passage is Mark's prelude to the feeding of the five thousand in 6:35-44. The missionaries have returned and offer Jesus an account of their activities. Jesus then decides that they need a rest after this period of ministry. With this, Mark is also preparing for the shepherd motif: 'they were like sheep without a shepherd' (v 34; see 1 Kgs 22:17).. In Ezekiel 34:15 and Psalm 23:2 the shepherd provides rest for his sheep. Mark then goes on to paint a vivid picture of the converging groups who travel on foot to meet Jesus.

Mark is clearly linking the feeding with the experience of Israel in the wilderness or desert after the Exodus. There the Lord provides water from the rock and feeds the Israelites with manna, a form of bread. Mark also underlines Jesus' compassion for the crowd. His initial reaction is not to feed the crowd with food but to teach them many things. Here Mark introduces another Old Testament motif. In the wisdom literature (see Prov 9:15; Sir 15:3) feeding and teaching are closely related and bread is associated with knowledge. Mark's audience thus learns that Jesus' teaching is as important for life as bread was for the Israelites in the wilderness or desert. Prompted by his sense of compassion, Jesus assumes the pastoral role of teaching.

Jesus Explains Ritual Purity (7:1-8, 14-15, 22-23)

In this episode clean and unclean relate to the Jewish concern for ritual purity. Here Jesus take exception to the principle of clean and unclean by stating: 'Nothing that enters one from outside can defile that person; but the things that come out from within are what defile' (v 15). For Jesus, holiness does not lie in the area of things but in the area of human conduct. It is the human heart that is ultimately the deciding factor. Nothing purely external separates a person from God.

Jesus also contrasts the Word of God and purely human law, citing

Isaiah 29:13. Here Jesus' opponents are guilty of disregarding God's commandment and clinging to human tradition (v 8). Ideology must always cede to divine commandment. For the Jesus of Mark, it is in the final analysis unreasonable and inhuman to obey simply because something is commanded.

Jesus Heals a Deaf Man with a Speech Impediment (7:31-37)

Mark uses this episode to depict his attitude towards the Gentiles. The geographical notice, namely, through the Gentile region of the Decapolis, serves to indicate his intent. The Gentiles, who at one time were deaf and speech-impaired toward God, are now able to hear God and do him obeisance. What God promised to Israel (see Isa 35:5-6) now holds true for the Gentiles.

The story of the cure of the deaf man with the speech impediment is different from Mark's usual miracle stories. Yet Jesus' actions were common among Greek and Jewish healers of the time. His actions are sacramental gestures, symbolizing the opening of the ears and the loosening of the tongue. By his use of the unique word for speech impediment (v 32), Mark is clearly citing Isaiah 35:6. Hence the messianic age has arrived in Jesus. Two other features are noteworthy: Jesus' groaning indicating great compassion for the sufferer and the unusual reaction of the people – their amazement is unbounded.

Here Jesus serves as a model for Mark's community. He reaches out to a Gentile audience and proclaims the good news by his mighty works. Jesus, therefore, joins the good news of the kingdom of God to the alleviation of human suffering and pain.

Journey to Jerusalem
(8:27 — 10:52)

After Peter's Confession
Jesus Makes His First Passion Prediction (8:27-35)

This passage marks a turning point in the self-revelation of Jesus. Up to this point Jesus has said nothing explicit about his messiahship. The scene as a whole is both a beginning, therefore, and an end. It is an end since it answers the question already suggested in so many of the preceding scenes: Is Jesus the Messiah? It is also also a beginning since it starts to qualify the type of Messiah, namely, a suffering Messiah. At the same time this passage is clearly linked with the immediately preceding cure of the blind man (8:22-26). The man only gradually regains his sight and, therefore, only gradually recognizes the real Jesus.

Mark has carefully structured this scene: (1) statement by Jesus; (2) misunderstanding of Jesus' statement; and (3) Jesus' clarification. The scene opens with the outsiders' view of Jesus' identity. After a few suggestions (John the Baptist, Elijah, one of the prophets) the insiders are invited to voice their opinion. Jesus' reaction to Peter's identification of him as Messiah (the Christ or Anointed One) is a sharp correction. Peter represents fallible followers who make the correct confession but then interpret their confession in the wrong way. To be sure, Jesus is the Messiah but only as the suffering Son of Man. Hence one properly recognizes Jesus when one sees him against the background of the cross. Anything else is simply a caricature. In the end Mark expands on this recognition by gathering some isolated sayings of Jesus. Discipleship means forgetting oneself - a radical forgetting symbolized by the desolation of the cross. One finds onself by losing oneself.

Jesus Is Transfigured (9:2-10)

Jesus' transfiguration is an epiphany, *i.e.*, a manifestation in which a divine figure or figures suddenly and unexpectedly appear and communicate something (in this instance the command to listen to Jesus). Jesus himself becomes such a heavenly figure (note his dazzling white clothes) in the company of Moses and Elijah who already belong to the heavenly world. According to 2 Kings 2:11 Elijah ascended into heaven in a whirlwind. Though Moses died on Mount Nebo (Deut 34:7), in first-century A.D. tradition he simply disappeared and returned to God.

While Moses and Elijah attained heavenly glory without experiencing death, Jesus will experience glory only after enduring death at the hands of the Roman authorities and his own people. Coming as it does after Jesus' first prediction of the passion, this event assures Jesus that his Father will exalt him. During the descent from the mountain Jesus demands silence about this episode until his resurrection.

At this point in his ministry Jesus realizes that his enemies will probably cause his death and hence he will not complete his mission. However, in the transfiguration he learns that he will achieve his mission through his suffering and death. Like the Suffering Servant (see Isa 52:13--53:12), Jesus is now aware that his death will not be the final act but that his Father will intervene on his behalf. The cross casts its shadow on the empty tomb.

Jesus Makes His Second Passion Prediction and Explains the Meaning of Greatness (9:30-37)

In this passage Mark continues his pattern of passion prediction, misunderstanding, and teaching about discipleship. Here the disciples not only fail to understand the statement about the suffering Son of Man but also do not intend to pursue any further instruction. They reflect the gravity of their misunderstanding by arguing among themselves who is the greatest.

Mark has carefully combined originally independent sayings of Jesus. The example of the little child is a fitting commentary on the issue of discipleship. In the Greco-Roman world the child was not the object of contemporary American endearment. Rather, being a child was precarious since the child was totally subject to the authority of the household head. As a result, the child symbolized powerlessness and total dependence on others. Here Jesus points out that the stance of the disciples should be the same. They should welcome the powerless and disenfranchised. This interprets first place in the kingdom, namely, being last of all and servant of all.

After Handling the Unaligned Exorcist Jesus Inveighs against Causing Temptation (9:38-43, 45, 47-48)

This passage is a series of sayings of Jesus that Mark found in his tradition and used to complement the second prediction of the passion. In the first saying (vv 39-40) Jesus resists all 'in-group' arrogance. God's power is not limited to the Jesus clientele. An outsider's exorcism in Jesus' name is not an attack on Jesus (see Acts 19:13-14). In the second saying (v 41) anyone who merely offers a drink of water will not be forgotten. No one has any right to despise a person who takes Jesus seriously. In the third saying (v 42) Jesus returns to the little ones (the simple believers - see 9:33-37). The millstone is a powerful image for expressing the heinousness of leading astray those who totally depend on God.

In a final cluster of sayings Jesus employs the image of mutilation to emphasize that obedience to God and sharing community with him have priority over everything else. 'Gehenna' comes from the Hebrew 'Valley of Worthlessness' – a valley just south of Jerusalem where human sacrifices had once been offered (see Jer 32:35). It later became Jerusalem's city dump - hence the reference to perpetual fire. The final verse borrows from Isaiah 66:24 that speaks of Gehenna's filth and smouldering fires. Once again, an apt image for the need to obey.

After Forbidding Divorce
Jesus Comments on the Role of Children (10:2-16)

In the dispute concerning divorce the Pharisees cite Deuteronomy 24:1-4 according to which, in their view, Moses gave permission for a man to divorce his wife. In reply, Jesus observes that Moses wrote the commandment because the people had failed to acknowledge the high demands of Genesis. According to those demands, marriage is a covenantal relationship in which loyalty is essential. Hence the will of the Creator takes precedence over the permissive rule of Moses. For Jesus, the question is not: What is allowed or permitted? But: What does God intend? For Jesus, the married couple is God's handiwork and therefore not even Moses' authority can be invoked to disrupt it.

The question scene back in the house (vv 10-12) shows that Mark is dealing with a Gentile audience since only in Roman law, not Jewish law, can a wife initiate divorce proceedings against a husband. These concluding verses reinforce what Jesus has already stated in his conversation with the Pharisees. A marriage after divorce is really adultery since the first marriage is still in effect.

In verses 13-16 Mark presents Jesus' attitude towards children. Children have the right attitude about entering the kingdom since they are willing to accept what is freely given. In order to share in the kingdom, one must have that same simplicity and accept the kingdom as a gift freely bestowed. The use of the verb 'to prevent' (v 14) may suggest that this passage played some part in the discussion of infant baptism (see Acts 8:37; 10:47).

Jesus Discusses Wealth and Discipleship (10:17-30)

In this passage Mark considers wealth a great threat to discipleship. The man in this account is obviously intent upon pursuing the path to eternal life. Once Jesus learns that he has observed the commandments from his youth, he challenges him to sell his possessions and give the income to the poor. Just prior to this demand, Mark observes that Jesus loves the man. Unfortunately Jesus' demand proves to be too exacting. Mark notes that his face falls and that he goes away, for he is extremely wealthy. At this juncture Jesus emphasizes the difficulty the rich experience in their attempt to enter the kingdom. It is like a camel trying to pass through the eye of a needle. This saying utterly astonishes the disciples who probably assume that wealth implies God's good pleasure. Their frustration expresses itself in their question about the possibility of salvation. Here Jesus responds that purely human efforts cannot attain salvation but that with God everything is possible.

Jesus' reply about salvation prompts Peter's question about the fate of the disciples who like himself have given up everything to follow him. In response, Jesus employs three categories: (1) home; (2) relatives including fathers; and (3) property. Significantly Jesus omits fathers among the rewards (v 30), thereby suggesting his rejection of a patriarchal style with its insistence on domination. Ironically perhaps but realistictally the hundredfold does not exclude persecutions.

Jesus Makes His Third Passion Prediction (10:35-45)

In the scene immediately preceding this passage Jesus has pronounced his third passion prediction, explaining at greater length the sufferings and humiliations he will endure. This then leads into a dialogue between Jesus and the two sons of Zebedee, James and John. Mark underlines the brothers' total misunderstanding by their request for the first places in the kingdom. This request compels Jesus to inquire about their ability to drink his cup and endure his baptism, i.e., to experience the pain and suffering that awaits him in Jerusalem. After their positive response Jesus assures them that they will indeed undergo everything that his cup and his baptism symbolize but that only God can assign positions in the kingdom.

At this point the other ten members of the Twelve become indignant at James and John. Jesus now seizes the occasion for further lessons on the nature of discipleship. Here Jesus describes the typical characteristics of Gentile civil authority: domination, lording it over subjects, making presence felt. However, in Jesus' community this is not to be the pattern at all. Rather, greatness is measured in service so that the leader assumes the position of slave of the community. Jesus proceeds to ground this fundamental teaching in his own person and demeanor, namely, freely given service. He did not come to be served but to serve. He adds: 'and to give his life as ransom for many' (v 45). 'Ransom' conjures up the image of releasing a captive or of a slave purchasing his or her freedom. Here 'many' (see Isa 53:12) carries the sense of 'all.'

Jesus Restores Sight to Blind Bartimaeus (10:46-52)

This scene in Mark climaxes Jesus' ministry of healing and teaching and provides the transition to his ministry in Jerusalem (11:1). In the other direction, it is a decided contrast to the request of James and John treated above and shows that the blind man Bartimaeus understands the nature of Jesus' messiahship. The story also has great symbolic value. Only those who experience Jesus' exaltation through suffering can have their eyes opened to his significance. To be sure, this demands great perseverance.

Hence Bartimaeus must overcome great odds in communicating his message and then in following Jesus down the way of discipleship. For Mark, the accent falls on the man's faith, not on the miracle. This is the type of faith that the true follower of Jesus should possess.

Jesus' Ministry in Jerusalem
(11:1 — 12:44)

Jesus Combines Love of God and Love of Neighbour as the Greatest Commandment (12:28-34)

This passage in Mark concerns the quest for the Great Commandment. The scribe refers to it as the first of all the commandments while Jesus labels it the greatest commandment. Out of the 248 commands and 365 prohibitions in the Torah Jesus chooses the two that give meaning and validity to all the others, namely, Deuteronomy 6:5 (love of God) and Leviticus 19:18 (love of neighbor). It is likely that Jesus was the first to bring together these two commandments of love.

Only in Mark does the scribe register his agreement with Jesus' response by paraphrasing it and commenting that the love commandments are more important than all burnt offerings and sacrifices. Only in Mark does Jesus remark that the scribe is not far from the kingdom of God.

What is especially significant about Jesus' combination is that he incorporated it into his own lifestyle. He welcomed human beings whom other despised (see 2:16-17; 10:14). As the scene in Gethsemane shows, he was obedient to his Father up to the very end.

Jesus Denounces the Scribes and Praises a Poor Widow's Contribution (12:38-44)

While Jesus' criticism of the scribes' egotistical posture and his praise of the widow's generosity can be taken separately, they are perhaps better understood as a contrast of two types of so-called religious persons. Jesus charges the scribes with: (1) ostentation in dress and greeting; (2) pursuit of places of honor in the synagogues and at banquets; (3) long-winded prayers; and (4) exploitation of the helpless (widows). The poor widow, on the other hand, deserves praise for her generous contribution to the temple treasury. Because she gives out of her poverty, she surpasses all the wealthy who contribute out of their surplus. For Mark, the widow emerges as an exemplar of genuine piety and generosity.

By having Jesus summon his disciples (v 43), Mark alerts his audience to the real meaning of this scene. According to Jesus' analysis the widow in effect gave herself whereas the others only gave something. By putting in two small coins worth a few cents, she surrendered herself entirely to God.

Eschatological Discourse (13:1-37)

Jesus Announces the Coming of the Son of Man and the Need for Vigilance (13:24-32)

'Eschatological' means 'last' – specifically it is a revelation or apocalypse regarding the mysteries of the future and/or the heavenly realm. In this discourse Jesus functions as the revealer. Seated on the Mount of Olives outside the Jerusalem temple, Jesus replies to a question put to him by four of his disciples about the end of the temple and the signs presaging its demise. Jesus then shifts from his prediction about the temple to discuss the cosmic signs that will usher in the coming of God's kingdom in its fullness. Mark's purpose in this chapter as a whole is twofold. First, he intends to show that when Jesus returns he will fulfill the Old Testament prophecies about the end. Second, Mark intends to warn his audience not to anticipate Jesus' second coming (parousia) by means of carefully calculated signs.

Using typically apocalyptic or revelatory language, Mark mentions the unmistakable cosmic signs that herald the arrival of Jesus. Here the title 'Son of Man' captures the central figure connected to the events associated with the full coming of God's kingdom (see Dan 7:13), such as the gathering of the elect from the four winds. The lesson from the fig tree (vv 28-31) may have originally served as a barometer of sorts for determining the coming of the end. However, here Mark exercises his pastoral care. In the final verse of this passage he asserts that only the Father, not even the Son, knows the exact timetable. What is needed, therefore, is watchful waiting. It is only fitting that Mark would conclude this eschatological discourse with the important pastoral directive to watch (13:37).

Jesus Reiterates the Need for Vigilance (13:33-37)

In this conclusion of the eschatological discourse Mark seeks to address the following question to his audience: Why the delay of Jesus' second coming, since he spoke of an imminent return? Although Mark himself may have anticipated an early return, he points out that prior to Jesus' return vigilance or watchfulness is required.

Mark has adapted the parable of the gatekeeper (vv 34-36) to underline the necessity of vigilance. The lord of the house is now Jesus who will return at the proper time. In turn, the gatekeeper represents the waiting community.

As the discourse winds down, Jesus bestows authority on his disciples (v 34: 'places his servants in charge'). However, authority implies service. In the troubling period prior to Jesus' return service assumes the form of vigilance that will prepare the community for the consummation of God's plan.

Jesus' Suffering, Death and Resurrection (14:1 – 16:20)

Mark Recounts Jesus' Passion and Death (14:1–15:47)

Mark's passion account is an exposé of the shocking facts that led to the death of Jesus. At the same time, however, it is an account that is full of paradox and mystery that are calculated to evoke from the reader the centurion's profession of faith: 'Truly this man was the Son of God!' (15:39).

In the garden scene (14:32-42) Mark underlines Jesus' intention to pray. Having selected the three special disciples to accompany him, he immediately begins to be troubled and distressed. His falling to the ground captures his anguished mental state. He addresses God as 'Abba' that Mark translates as 'Father.' This address connotes Jesus' sense of intimacy and familiarity. He asks his Father to remove the cup, the symbol of his excruciating ordeal but quickly adds: 'but not what I will but what you will' (14:36). His three companions, however, provide no relief for they have fallen asleep. Jesus returns to his prayer and goes back once again to find the disciples fast asleep. After a third period of prayer and his return to the comatose disciples he solemnly announces that the hour of betrayal is at hand.

In the arrest scene (14:43-52) Mark paints a very brusque picture. A mob with swords and clubs converges on Jesus. While Jesus reads this as the arrest of a brigand, he addresses no word to Judas or the disciple who struck the high priest's servant. In the end Jesus is abandoned by all, even by a young man forced to flee naked.

In the Jewish trial (14:53-65) the outcome is not the establishing of Jesus' guilt but the revelation of his unique dignity. To 'the Christ, the son of the Blessed One' Jesus adds a combination of Son of Man (see Dan 7:13) and 'seated at the right hand' (see Ps 110:1). However, this revelation does not provoke homage, only the cry of blasphemy that then leads to abuse,

Peter's denial (14:66-72), and the resolve to take Jesus to Pilate (15:1).

In the Roman trial (15:2-20) Pilate is disconcerted by Jesus' silence. Since it is the trial of the King of the Jews (repeated no less than four times), Jesus must get the 'royal' treatment: (1) purple mantle; (2) a crown; (3) the 'homage' of the soldiers (15:16-19).

In the crucifixion and death scenes (15:21-41) the title 'the King of the Jews' is placed between the two notices of crucifixion (15:25,27). The taunts of the people refer to Jesus' prophecy about the temple but in 15:38 the temple loses its significance when the veil is torn. The chief priests and scribes mock him as 'the Christ, the King of Israel' (15:31) but in 15:39 the centurion confesses Jesus as much more, namely, 'the Son of God.' The picture is indeed bleak, that of a man seemingly deserted by his Father (15:34: 'My God, my God').

In the burial scene (15:42-47) the infamy begins to disappear to some extent as a member of the Sanhedrin offers to give Jesus something of a decent burial. While Mark attests the reality of the death, he also suggests the paradox of Easter morning by naming the two Marys again (15:47; see 15:40).

Mark Narrates the Last Supper, the Eucharist, and the Departure to the Mount of Olives (14.12-16,22-26)

This passage consists of three components: (1) preparations for the Passover meal (14:12-16); (2) the institution of the Eucharist (14:22-25); and (3) departure to the Mount of Olives (14:26). It is not clear whether the Last Supper was a Passover meal or not. In any event Mark deliberately ties Jesus' death to the Passover. The ancient feast celebrating the liberation of the Israelites from Egypt now commemorates the liberation from death.

In the institution of the Eucharist Mark emphasizes Jesus' words, actions, and interpretations of the bread and wine. Both the bread and the wine constitute the very presence of Jesus that establishes a covenant relationship. When Jesus distributes the broken pieces of bread to the disciples, he symbolizes their sharing in his self-offering. 'The blood of the covenant' (14:24) alludes to Exodus 24:8 in which Moses ratifies the covenant on Sinai by sprinkling the people with the blood of the communion offerings. Jesus' own blood will ratify this new covenant. By drinking the cup, the disciples enter into this covenant relationship with Jesus. Jesus also interprets the shedding of his blood for 'many,' a Semitic expression meaning 'all.' This expression together with the 'pouring out' is a link to the Suffering Servant of Isaiah 52:13--53:12. Eucharist is thus seen as a new source of life by which one shares community with Jesus. At the same time there is also an element of anticipation. The disciples are to look forward to that final meal over which Jesus will preside in God's kingdom.

A Young Man Explains to the Women why the Tomb is Empty (16:1-7)

Unlike the other evangelists, Mark does not mention the women's execution of the young man's command to tell Jesus' disciples and Peter the astounding news of the empty tomb. Verse 8 (not in this passage) cites the women's fear for their noncompliance. Thus not only the male disciples but also the female disciples have failed Jesus. One way to explain this debacle is to shift the emphasis from human failure to divine intervention. In the final analysis, whereas all human beings fail, God succeeds. Despite Jesus' cry of abandonment (15:34), God has intervened by raising him from the dead. In keeping with Jesus' promise in 14:28 and the young man's promise in 16:7, the disciples will encounter the risen Jesus in Galilee. This encounter rests, not on human success but on divine initiative.

According to Mark the women bring perfumed oils to anoint the body of Jesus. Much to their surprise, they find that the stone at the entrance of the tomb has been rolled back. (This is a 'divine passive,' *i.e.*, God has actually rolled back the stone.) At this point Mark notes that the stone was very large. Then a young man dressed in a white robe functions as a so-called interpreting angel. In apocalyptic literature it is the task of such angels to unravel divine mysteries. After noting the women's fright, the young man interprets the reason for the empty tomb, namely, the resurrection of Jesus.

The angel or young man proclaims the Christian belief in the death and resurrection of Jesus. He is 'Jesus of Nazareth' - a title that Mark uses both in the beginning and end of his gospel. Jesus is also the crucified one. Yet the paradox is that death gives way to glory: 'He has been raised!'

The Risen Lord Commissions the Eleven and Is Taken up into Heaven (16:15-20)

This passage is part of the longer ending of the Gospel of Mark (16:9-20). Although regarded as part of the canonical Scriptures, this longer ending is not the work of Mark. It is a summary of the postresurrectional appearances of Jesus and reflects traditions common to Luke 24 and John 20. The author of this longer ending resolves the enigma of the original ending of Mark (16:8) according to which the women failed to carry out their commission.

After reproaching the Eleven for their lack of faith, Jesus announces the universal mission (v 15: 'every creature'). According to verse 16 salvation depends on faith in the good news and the acceptance of baptism. The proclamation, therefore, provokes a response of either belief or disbelief. The signs (vv 17-18) demonstrate the establishment of the kingdom.

Verse 19 uses the language of Elijah's ascension (see 2 Kgs 2:11) and the Davidic king's divine adoption ('God's right hand' - see Ps 110:1) to describe the exaltation of Jesus on the day of Easter itself. This exaltation legitimates the use of the title 'Lord Jesus,' frequent in Acts but nowhere else in the gospels. It is significant that the exalted Lord cooperates with the Eleven in their proclamation of the Word. The exaltation, therefore, means the ongoing involvement of the heavenly Lord in the activities of his earthly community.

Concluding Reflections on the Gospel of Mark

For Mark's audience the Jesus of this gospel becomes a paradigm of hope. In this Jesus they can discover themselves because they too have experienced the pain reflected in Mark's Suffering Servant. Like the Jesus of Mark's passion predictions they have encountered persecution, in some instances persecution that has led to death. But, as the gospel closes, they can begin to grasp the poignant mystery of the empty tomb. Their God has also acted on their behalf by raising Jesus from the dead and, with Jesus, their hope.

This audience can also rally to Jesus' frontal attack on the demonic power of evil. Having experienced the brutality and inhumanity of Roman justice, they too have come to grips with cosmic evil. They can see themselves depicted in Jesus' exorcisms. His all-powerful involvement will never permit Satan and his minions to have the final say. In this Jesus they can envision the victory of good over evil, of humanity over inhumanity, of hope over crushing despair.

In addition to the exorcisms, this audience finds consolation in Jesus' conquest of human pain and suffering. Like Peter's mother-in-law, the man with the withered hand, and blind Bartimaeus, they discover in this Jesus one who wages an incessant campaign against everything that oppresses and depresses the human spirit. They can walk with heads held high because this Son of Man has deigned to enter their pain and provide the soothing balm of empathy.

This audience can recognize in the Markan Jesus one like themselves. He too reveals flashes of anger when basic human values are in danger of being snuffed out. He also manifests extreme compassion for all those considered outsiders. He welcomes society's rejects and pariahs to table fellowship with himself. He perceives the needs of women and vehemently refuses to shun them. In such displays of common humanity the audience recognizes itself.

Last but certainly not least, this audience identifies with Mark's description of the all too fallible disciples. While they acknowledge Jesus' call to follow him on this road, they know the hazards and pitfalls of this trek since the cross casts its shadow everywhere. They can resonate with Judas the betrayer and Peter the denier. They can see themselves in the obtuse Twelve who seem to excel in misunderstanding. At the same time they can appreciate the patience and tolerance that Jesus constantly demonstrates. Though abandoned by his disciples, he learns to forgive as he encounters them in Galilee after his resurrection. This audience has dared to learn from the failure of fellow humans and the unfathomable folly of the cross.

The Jesus of Matthew

The Setting of the Gospel of Matthew

The Roman destruction of Jerusalem and its temple in the year 70A.D. was nothing less than traumatic for the Jewish people. They now faced the daunting task of preserving Jewish tradition and identity in the absence of political hegemony and religious symbolism. The destruction also raised doubts about God's election of Israel and his sense of fidelity. There was no such thing as a monolithic uniformity in religion. Even prior to the destruction Judaism was diverse with a coalition of sects and movements. The synagogues throughout the country reflected divisions and a variety of approaches to Jewish life. It was also a period in which Judaism and Christianity had not yet gone their separate ways.

Along with the scribes (the lay legal experts) and the Pharisees (a religious sect) the author Matthew endeavored to retain and continue Jewish identity and values. The Gospel of Matthew was only one of several Jewish responses to the trauma of 70A.D. In this melee Matthew strove to show how the Jewish tradition is best preserved in the Jewish-Christian context. He resolved to assist his fellow Jewish-Christians in understanding that their faith was indeed consistent with Jewish heritage.

To achieve this goal, Matthew presented Jesus the Jew as the faithful interpreter of the Torah. He pictured Jesus as one whose whole life was in perfect harmony with the Jewish Scriptures. It would perhaps be more accurate to say that these Scriptures were in perfect harmony with the lifestyle and accomplishments of Jesus. To this end, Matthew frequently used fulfillment quotations from Israel's sacred texts to establish the continuity between Jewish heritage and the Christian movement. For example, on Palm Sunday, when Jesus rides into Jerusalem, he writes: 'This happened so that what had been spoken through the prophet (Zech 9:9) might be fulfilled: 'Say to daughter Zion, "Behold, your king comes to you, … "'' (21:5). For Matthew, there is a long line of continuity between the Jewish Scriptures and Jesus.

The Jesus of Matthew is pre-eminently the Teacher. Matthew creates this image by his structural architecture and use of sources. While borrowing Mark's account of Jesus along with its tripartite structure (Galilean ministry, journey to Jerusalem, and Jerusalem ministry culminating in death and resurrection), he places five great speeches on the lips of Jesus (occurring throughout chapters 5 to 7, 10, 13, 18, and 24 to 25). Matthew then supplements these main blocks of speeches with narrative blocks. In addition to Mark, Matthew also uses a collection of sayings and his own special material. The sayings source is called 'Q' from the German *Quelle* meaning 'source' that is culled from the 220 to 235 verses or parts of verses common to Matthew and Luke but not found in Mark, e.g., the Lord's Prayer. Matthew's own special source is labelled 'M,' *e.g.*, the infancy narrative. By his masterful use of these sources Matthew has created the gospel of Jesus the Teacher.

Most scholars generally place the time of composition of Matthew between 80 to 90A.D. One likely place of composition is Antioch in Syria. This city had a large population of both Jews and non-Jews who spoke and wrote Hellenistic Greek.

Jesus' Origins
(1:1 – 2:25)

Matthew Provides Jesus' Genealogy and Narrates His Birth (1:1-25)

Matthew's genealogy situates Jesus in the history of Israel. He is both son of Abraham and royal son of David. As such, he can appeal to both the Jewish-Christian members of Matthew's community and the Gentile members (see Gen 22:18 where all the nations of the earth shall find blessing in Abraham's descendants). Matthew thus demonstrates how God has provided for all humanity. He works this out artistically by arranging three sections of fourteen generations. He also introduces four women into the genealogy, where the combination of irregularity and divine intervention prepares for Mary. By means of the genealogy, therefore, Jesus belongs to a history and a people.

Verses 18-25 are an expanded footnote that explains the irregularity of the genealogy. If Jesus has no human father, then how can he be called 'son of David' (v 1)? The footnote explains that Joseph is perplexed by Mary's pregnancy but that because of the angel's revelation he is willing to accept legal paternity. Hence in verse 20 Joseph is addressed as 'son of David.' Moreover, the final verse states categorically: 'and he named him Jesus' (v 25).

Matthew rereads the text of Isaiah 7:14 in light of Jesus' Davidic origin, using the Greek Old Testament text, i.e., 'virgin' instead of 'maiden.' Jesus will be Emmanuel - 'God with us.' In turn, Matthew binds his whole gospel together by having Jesus promise in the very last verse (28:20): 'I am with you always.' The generous response of the couple makes initially possible the abiding presence of Jesus.

The Magi Visit Jesus and His Mother in Bethlehem (2:1-12)

This passage consists of two scenes. In the first (vv 1-6) the magi arrive from the east in Jerusalem and are then directed to Bethlehem. The scene closes with the citation of Micah 5:1 and 2 Samuel 5:2 speaking of Bethlehem and the Davidic king. In the second (vv. 7-12) the magi go to Bethlehem, worship the king, offer him gifts, and leave for their home by another route. Like the shepherds in Luke 2:1-20, the magi are directed to the infant, recognize him, and then leave as quickly as they came.

Magus covers a wide variety of fields such as astronomy, fortune telling, etc. The translation 'astrologer' seems to fit best here because of the star. For Matthew, these magi represent the best of pagan religion, for they have come to discover Jesus by a natural means, namely, a star. At a time when many Gentiles were accepting Jesus, Jews were rejecting him (see 21:42-43). Matthew points out to his community that the presence of Gentiles was part of God's plan all along. In this passage, therefore, he proposes a twofold reaction to the good news of God's revelation. Pagans (the magi with a star) are the first to come and pay homage, whereas the Jews (Herod and the chief priests and scribes) with the Scriptures reject him (see 27:1,37). Matthew, therefore, tells this story with a view to the ministry of Jesus and especially the needs of his community.

Matthew develops this account by means of a popular reflection on the Scriptures. He uses Isaiah 60:1 that speaks of a rising light as well as Isaiah 60:5-6 that mentions caravans from the Arabian desert loaded with gold and frankincense. He also cites Psalm 72:10-11 that refers to the kings of Sheba and Seba bringing tribute and paying homage to the Davidic king. He also combines Micah 5:1 and 2 Samuel 5:2 to his own advantage, making Bethlehem a significant town and stressing the Davidic role of shepherding the people of Israel respectively. Finally he borrows from the story of Balaam (see Num 22--24). This magus was a non-Israelite who came from the east and made a prediction about a star rising from Jacob and a man standing forth from Israel (Greek text of Num 24:17). In the first century A.D., Balaam's star already had a messianic interpretation.

Matthew Recounts the Flight into Egypt and the Return to Israel (2:13-15.19-23)

Matthew's story of the flight into Egypt (vv 13-15) and the return to Israel (vv 19-23) may contain some historical kernels. Egypt, the classical land of refuge in the Old Testament, was not far from Bethlehem, the home of Mary and Joseph according to 2:11. Moreover, the character of Herod is consistent with Jewish sources. However, what is evident is Matthew's own use of the materials.

According to Matthew, Jesus re-lives the story of Israel in his own life. Like Israel, he must leave Canaan and go down to Egypt. Like Israel, he must return from Egypt to Canaan. In verse 15 Matthew cites Hosea 11:1 according to which he sees Jesus as God's Son coming out of Egypt as the new Israel. In verse 20 he quotes Exodus 4:19, the words of the Lord to Moses to return to Egypt from Midian. Jesus is the new Moses since he is rescued from Herod as Moses was rescued from Pharaoh. In verse 23 Matthew cites a prophetic text that says that Jesus will be called a Nazarene (see Isa 4:2; Judg 16:17). While explaining Nazareth as Jesus' new home, the text also presents him as dedicated to the Lord like Samson and the Davidic branch.

In these two scenes Joseph is the silent but obedient servant. Matthew ranges him with the Gentile magi and faithful Jews. While the Jewish authorities reject, Joseph accepts.

Beginning of the Ministry of Jesus
(3:1 – 4:25)

John the Baptist Preaches in the Desert of Judea (3:1-12)

Following Mark, Matthew presents the Baptist as a prophet after the manner of Elijah (see 2 Kgs 1:8). His prophetic message is repentance, i.e., the human response to God's saving presence by a reversal of human standards and the adoption of God's ways (see 16:23). 'Kingdom' implies that, like the ideal king of the ancient Near East, God will provide for all the needs of his people. The rite of baptism symbolizes this radically new way of thinking/acting.

Whereas Luke has the Baptist address the crowds, Matthew has him speak directly to the unlikely union of Pharisees and Sadducees. They compose the united front that will also oppose Jesus. The Baptist will not tolerate any insistence on blood ties (v 9: 'We have Abraham as our father'). As the magi account shows, Matthew's community is also open to the Gentiles. This hardened opposition is also a warning to the leaders in Matthew's own community (see 7:19).

In this scene the focus of attention is on 'the one who is coming after me' (v 11). John is slave (v 11: 'carry his sandals'), not master. Whereas

John baptizes in water, 'the mightier one' (v 11) will communicate the Spirit. Although 'spirit and fire' originally referred to divine judgment, Christian tradition eventually interpreted the phrase in terms of the Spirit.

John Baptises Jesus in the Jordan (3:13-17)

Matthew's baptism scene does not emphasize the baptism as much as the identity of Jesus at the beginning of his public ministry. Here in Matthew Jesus comes to be baptized in order to obey God's command (v 15: 'to fulfill all righteousness'). This is Matthew's explanation of why the superior was baptized by the inferior. Thus only in Matthew do we find a dialogue between Jesus and John in which John already knows that Jesus is the one about whom he has been prophesying.

Unlike Mark, Matthew has made Jesus' experience of the Father and his plan a public event. Thus 'the heavens were opened' (v 16) rather than Mark's 'he saw the heavens being torn open' (1:10). Also 'This is my beloved Son' (v 17) rather than Mark's 'You are my beloved Son' (1:11). This divine manifestation (theophany) has links with the Old Testament, especially Isaiah 63:11-19 in which the prophet speaks of the Exodus, the division of the waters, and the descent of the spirit. The final verse connects the rending of the heavens with God's coming down.

'This is my beloved Son, with whom I am well pleased' comes from the first Suffering Servant Song (Isa 42:1). Matthew views Jesus as the Lord's Servant, the recipient of the Spirit (see 12:18-21). In Matthew's hands, Jesus is aware not only of his intimate relationship with the Father but also of his acceptance of the Father's will, i.e., his vocation for Israel. The temptation scene (4:1-11) will test Jesus' acceptance of that will.

Jesus Is Tempted in the Desert (4:1-11)

Matthew's testing of Jesus account (that he takes from 'Q') contrasts the infidelity of Israel in the wilderness with the fidelity of Jesus to his mission. The first testing cites Deuteronomy 8:3 and refers to Exodus 16:1-15 where Israel grumbles against the Lord and receives the manna. The testing consists in inaugurating the kingdom by catering to the popular demand for a repetition of the wilderness miracles. In essence, this means manipulating people and, therefore, Jesus rejects it. The second testing quotes Deuteronomy 6:16 and goes back to Exodus 17:1-7, the Israelites' complaint to Moses because of lack of water. The devil's use of Psalm 91 suggests a messianic figure who would win popular acclaim by leaping from the parapet of the temple. If Jesus were to do so, he would force his Father's hand to perform a miracle. Unlike Israel, Jesus rejects the offer. The third testing cites Deuteronomy 6:13 and looks to the temptation to idolatry that Israel would experience upon reaching the Promised Land. Jesus is tempted to adore Satan in person, since the world and its power are in his domain. Jesus, however, refuses. His kingdom will not come about in this way.

By speaking of forty days and nights (see Exod 34:28) as well as the very high mountain (Mt Nebo – see Deut 34:1), Matthew establishes a Moses-Jesus typology. More important, Matthew depicts Jesus rejecting the popular notion of a political, temporal Messiah. Only later will Jesus develop a clearer notion of mission. Ultimately that mission will narrow down to Calvary.

Jesus Begins His Ministry, Calls His First Disciples and Ministers to Great Crowds (4:12-23)

This passage consists of three components: (1) Jesus' return to Galilee after his baptism (vv 12-17); (2) the call of the first four disciples (vv 18-22); and (3) a summary of his Galilean campaign of teaching and healing (v 23). In the first section Matthew establishes further connections between Jesus and the Baptist. Like John, Jesus will also be handed over (see 17:22; 27:2,26). Jesus also preaches the same message as John regarding repentance and the nearness of the kingdom. (Matthew prefers to describe this kingdom as 'of heaven,' not 'of God.') Abandoning human standards and acceptance of God's way ('repent') are the only adequate responses to this invitation. In order to ground Jesus' return in obedience to God's will, Matthew quotes Isaiah 8:23–9:1, an expression of hope after the Assyrian conquest in 732 B.C. 'Galilee of the Gentiles' suggests Matthew's overture to non-Jews (see 28:19).

In the call narrative Matthew follows his source Mark. The four disciples react immediately to the authoritative call of Jesus. Like Mark, Matthew does not spare them the cost of discipleship, namely, abandonment of both jobs and families.

In the summary of Jesus' teaching and healing all around Galilee, Matthew is preparing for his first great speech (the Sermon on the Mount) that follows immediately. Matthew also establishes Jesus' appeal to the Galileans and their decidedly positive response.

Speech 1: The Sermon on the Mount (5:1 – 7:29)

Jesus Introduces the Beatitudes (5:1-12a)

This passage has two main sections: (1) setting (vv 1-2); and (2) the Beatitudes (vv 3-12). The setting of the mountain is significant since a mountain often serves as a place of divine revelation in the Bible. Like Moses, Jesus finds himself on a mountain. But unlike Moses who receives the revelation, Jesus here gives the revelation. Jesus' sitting posture indicates that he is indeed a teacher. The people gathered about him represent Israel as a whole that is invited to discover in Jesus' teaching the authentic interpretation of God's will in the Torah.

In setting out the plan for the kingdom, Jesus first introduces the Beatitudes. They describe the qualities of happiness or blessedness that the practitioners of these virtues will eventually receive in God's perfect kingdom. Unlike Luke who has four beatitudes, Matthew has nine. Four of the nine stress a passive attitude (vv 3-6), while the next four stress a passive attitude (vv 7-10). Matthew's Beatitudes conclude with a longer final beatitude on persecution (vv 11-12).

Unlike Luke who uses the second person and portrays the actually poor, etc., Matthew uses the third person (see Ps 1:1) and applies his Beatitudes to more spiritual and moral needs. The first beatitude looks back to the humble of the land in the prophet Zephaniah. By accepting God's view, such people will possess the kingdom. To those who mourn because of their human condition, God promises consolation on the last day. The lowly, i.e., those who do not assert their power, the unassuming like Jesus (see Ps 37:11), will enter the kingdom as well. Those hungering and thirsting for the right covenantal relationship between God and people (righteousness) will be satisfied. The merciful who exclude no one will not find themselves excluded. Those who have an undivided heart, one totally given over to God's outlook, will experience God in paradise. Those who remove the barriers to genuine human living (the peacemakers) will learn on the last day that they are truly God's daughters and sons. Those who continue to suffer by accepting God's views will be indeed worthy of the kingdom. Finally those who suffer harassment because of allegiance to Jesus are in the tradition of the prophets and will have a comparable reward.

Jesus Describes His Disciples by Using Images of Salt and Light (5:13-16)

In the last beatitude (5:11-12), Matthew spoke of the persecuted. By joining two originally separate sayings (salt and light), Matthew paradoxicaly addresses these persecuted as the hope of the world, namely, those who follow Jesus faithfully.

Salt was an invaluable commodity in the ancient world. The disciple of Jesus is to be to the world what salt was to the ancients. The lifestyle of Jesus' followers is thus vital for the world's welfare. If their lifestyle should cease to be genuine, then they would be as useless as flat salt. An unfaithful disciple is an insipid disciple.

Light also exemplifies the public character of discipleship. In the one-room, windowless Palestinian house, the light from the lamp was very important for all in the household. The disciple also lives for others. Again, they are as public as a city on a hill – their presence cannot be mistaken. In the final verse (v 16) Matthew returns to the light image and establishes a system of links for the disciple. People in general will notice their lifestyle and connect that with their heavenly Father. Thus discipleship that is fundamentally concern for others is grounded in the glory of God.

Jesus Discusses the Mosaic Law and Contrasts That Law with His Own Interpretation (5:17-37)

The first four verses of this passage establish the relationship between Jesus' teaching and the Torah. Jesus in no way nullifies the Mosaic Law. Rather, he fulfills it. The righteousness, i.e., the moral living out of God's will, demands that the disciple go beyond the legalistic attitude of the scribes and Pharisees. It is not a question of a better type of Pharisaism. It is a question, rather, of the disciple's total self-giving to God and neighbor.

Verses 21-48 are a series of six antitheses (opposition/contrast) that exemplify the principle propounded in verse 20 about the righteousness expected of Jesus' disciples. This section contrasts what God once said with what Jesus now says. The first antithesis (vv 21-26) radicalizes the Mosaic prohibition against murder. Anger towards one's neighbor is as detestable as murder, since the neighbor's dignity must be respected. Reconciliation with one's sister or brother is the only way to be reconciled with God.

The second antithesis (vv 27-30) enlarges the Mosaic prohibition against adultery to include lustful looks and thoughts. The woman is not a sex object – she is a person to be accorded her rightful dignity. Verses 29-30 about tearing out one's right eye and cutting off one's right hand are metaphorical language: the saving of the entire person at the final judgment deserves any and every effort now.

The third antithesis (vv 31-32) revokes the Mosaic permission regarding divorce. 'Unlawful marriage' may refer to incestuous marriages already forbidden in the Torah (see Lev 18:6-18) and, therefore, not necessarily a departure from Jesus' strong stand against divorce.

The fourth antithesis (vv 33-37) deals with oaths and vows. Here Matthew has Jesus totally reject such Mosaic practices. To call God as a witness is to violate God's majesty. The Jesus of Matthew thereby rejects all human efforts to control or manipulate God. Instead of swearing at all, one should limit oneself to a simple yes or no.

Jesus Proposes Two More Contrasts with the Torah (5:38-48)

In the fifth antithesis (vv 38-42) Jesus revokes the Mosaic command regarding proportionate retaliation. In its place he does not propose a new program, for in him the end of human society has arrived. All human legal systems (e.g., going to court) and human checks and balances (e.g., a slap for a slap) must go. The principle advocated by Jesus is to yield one's rights in view of strict claims (e.g., walking the extra mile). In his sixth and final antithesis (vv 43-48) Jesus does not reject Leviticus 19:18 (the Torah did not command hatred of one's neighbour). In redefining the notion of neighbour, Jesus simply eliminates all limitations on love because that is precisely how the Father acts. Thus the Father provides for everyone because he refuses to exclude anyone from his love. The you-scratch-my-back-and-I'll-scratch-yours attitude of the pagans and the IRS ('tax collectors') is declared unworthy of a disciple of Jesus. The manner of the Father ('perfect') must become the manner of the disciple.

Jesus Speaks about False Gods (Money) and the Role of Providence (6:24-34)

This section of the Sermon on the Mount revolves around verse 24, the worship of the true God or the worship of false gods (worldly possessions). The only options are love or hate. What Matthew expects from his community is an attitude of trust.

Matthew does not rule out concern for material needs. Rather, he invites his audience to liberate itself from slavery to the anxieties of daily needs. The only means of liberation is total trust in God as provider. This allows the disciple to maintain the following priorities: life and body as gifts for which food and clothes are merely means.

If God feeds the birds and clothes the flowers of the field, both of which belong to this passing world, with how much more care will he provide for the needs of his people? Matthew then scolds his audience (v 30: 'O you of little faith') for they are asking the wrong questions, questions that smack of the pagans and their worship of this passing world. Without disparaging the quest for physical needs (v 33: 'seek first'), Matthew suggests that this is the right question: How can I seek God's saving plan ('kingdom') in my circumstances? Using a proverb (v 34: 'Sufficient for a day is its own evil'), the Jesus of Matthew teaches that the future is in God's hands. The only quest should be for today's bread.

Jesus Describes Two Different Types of Disciples (7:21-27)

In this conclusion of the Sermon on the Mount the Jesus of Matthew describes two different types of disciples. In verse 21 he begins his attack on the charismatic fakers in the community. At worship they enthusiastically cry out: 'Lord, Lord!' but in practice they amount to nothing. Like Israel, Matthew's community is called upon to do God's will. On the day of judgment prophecies, exorcisms, and miracles will count for nothing - doing the Father's will is the ultimate criterion. It is not enough to say, one must also do.

Verses 24-27 are Matthew's parable where the accent is now hearing/doing, not hearing/not-doing. Hearing/doing is the characteristic of the wise person. Hearing/not-doing is the mark of the foolish person. The image is one of a serious rain and wind storm. The hearers/doers survive because the house is built on a solid rock foundation. The hearers/non-doers do not survive because the house is built on sandy ground. To survive the final judgment, the disciple must be a hearer/doer.

Jesus' Mighty Deeds
(8:1 – 9:38)

Jesus Calls Matthew to Discipleship and Defends His Practice of Table Fellowship (9:9-13)

In the Sermon on the Mount Matthew has created a striking portrait of Jesus as mighty in word. In 8:1–9:38 he presents a Jesus who is also mighty in deeds. This passage serves as an interlude of sorts between the second series of miracle stories (8:18–9:8) and the third series (9:18-34).

This passage reveals the reaction to the healing of the paralytic (9:1-8) that underlines Jesus' mercy and forgiveness of sins. Because the tax collectors worked for the hated Roman equivalent of the IRS and had a reputation for injustice, the call of Matthew is a parade example of the gratituitous nature of the call to discipleship (v 9: 'Follow me'). Unlike his source Mark, Matthew changes the name of the tax collector from 'Levi' to 'Matthew,' thus identifying him as one of the Twelve (see 10:3).

The Pharisees become upset because Jesus eats with the hated IRS and the non-observant Jews ('sinners'). Here the Pharisees approach the disciples of Jesus rather than Jesus himself. Overhearing them, however, Jesus first reacts by citing a proverb, namely, that the sick, not the healthy, require a physician (and Jesus is one). Secondly, Jesus quotes Hosea 6:6 ('I desire mercy, not sacrifice'). (In Matthew 'sacrifice' connotes a program of ritual purity and Sabbath observance proposed by the opponents of Matthew's community.) Jesus' invitation (v 13: 'come to call'), however, accentuates the role of mercy. Matthew also implies that, if the so-called righteous reject Jesus' table fellowship with tax collectors and sinners, they may find themselves excluded from the final banquet, namely, the kingdom.

Speech 2: The Missionary Discourse (10:1-42)

Jesus Has Compassion on the Crowds, Chooses the Twelve and Sends Them on Mission (9:36–10:8)

The first three verses of this passage look forward to the missionary discourse in chapter 10. The sight of the crowds moves Jesus to compassion. These crowds resemble helpless, exhausted sheep who are deprived of a shepherd (see Num 27:17; 1 Kgs 22:17). Jesus proceeds to read the scene in terms of a great harvest (a symbol of final judgment) in which his disciples will play a key role by bringing his message to others. At the same time, given the scarcity of laborers, one must beg the Father, the lord of the harvest, to provide.

Matthew 10:1-4 is the introduction to the missionary discourse. Here Jesus provides an answer to the prayer of 9:38 by summoning the twelve disciples and sharing his mission with them. In verse 1 Jesus empowers them to carry out what he has exemplified in chapters 8 and 9, namely, exorcisms and healings. Only here (v 2) does Matthew call the Twelve 'apostles' (a term meaning one sent or commissioned). For Matthew they symbolize all later disciples and, more significantly, the later leaders of the community.

The Twelve are to go only to the lost sheep of the house of Israel, not the Gentiles (28:16-20, however, mention a universal mission). The Twelve are to announce the arrival of the kingdom, just as Jesus did (4:17). With the exception of teaching (see 4:23), the Twelve carry out the same work as Jesus in chapters 4 to 9. Since the powers conferred by Jesus on the Twelve are gratuitous, their use of such powers is also to be gratuitous.

Jesus Exhorts His Missionaries to be Fearless (10:26-33)

In verses 17-25 of his missionary discourse Mathew has described the opposition to and persecution of the disciples. In this passage he takes up the task of exhorting them to be fearless. Indeed he repeats this exhortation no less than three times (vv 26, 28, 31). Notwithstanding such hostility, the good news will go forth. These private instructions to the disciples are to be made public on mission. The disciples should not fear the destroyer of the body but the destroyer of the whole person in eternal damnation (unlike Luke 12:4, Matthew distinguishes body and soul).

The fear described here should elicit total confidence in a loving and concerned Father. The disciples are infinitely more valuable than the cheapest bird (sparrow) for which God provides abundantly. Indeed the Father knows even the smallest details about them, even the number of hairs on their heads. Hence they are to bear witness before implacable courtrooms. Then in the final courtroom scene Jesus will provide them with the necessary testimony. However, to disown Jesus before human tribunals is to have Jesus disown them before the heavenly tribunal.

Jesus Concludes the Missionary Discourse (10:37-42)

This passage is the conclusion of Matthew's missionary discourse. In verses 37-39 he develops the personal cost of discipleship. In verses 40-42 he offers the promise of rewards. By definition the missionary must be a partner to the mission and fate of Jesus. The way of the Master is the way of the disciple.

To be worthy of Jesus, one cannot love family members more than Jesus. The cross thereby becomes the symbol of the lengths to which the committed disciple may have to go. In the following of Jesus no price is too high. Matthew then offers the paradox of Christian discipleship. By seeking yourself, you lose yourself; by losing yourself, you find yourself. This is nothing less than a formulation of the death/resurrection experience of Jesus.

In verses 40-42 Matthew lines up possible recipients of the disciple's dedication: (1) apostles; (2) prophets; (3) righteous people; and (4) little ones, most likely the ordinary members of the community (see 18:10). Not to overlook them is to be duly rewarded.

The Rejection of Jesus
(11:1 – 12:50)

Jesus Receives the Baptist's Messengers
and Testifies to His Greatness (11:2-11)

Chapters 11-12 consider Israel's rejection of its Messiah. In these chapters questions, disputations, counterattacks, etc. take center stage while the number of miracles decreases and opposition of enemies increases. This opening passage consists of two units: (1) John's question to Jesus (vv 2-6) and Jesus' evaluation of John (vv 7-11).

In 3:11-12 Matthew presented John the Baptist as a fiery eschatological preacher of judgment. After his imprisonment (14:1-12) John heard reports of Jesus' preaching, healing, and teaching. The manner of Jesus raised doubts in the mind of the Baptist. He felt constrained to send a delegation to Jesus to learn if Jesus really was the Messiah (v 3: 'the one who is to come').

Jesus' reply is to point to the teaching and miracles of chapters 5-9. The high point is that the poor have the good news proclaimed to them (see Isa 61:1-2). Although this is not John's conception of messiahship, it is Jesus'. Jesus concludes the first unit with a gentle rebuke: 'blessed is the one who takes no offense at me' (v 6). The Baptist is not to fall from faith but to accept Jesus as the fulfillment of the Father's plan, not his own.

In the second unit Jesus lauds the Baptist but, as regards the kingdom, limits him. John was not simply marking time along the Jordan. He did not aim to please his listeners, especially Herod Antipas. He aimed to please God because he was a prophet. As a result, John landed in Herod's prison, not his palace. John is the messenger that the prophet Malachi spoke of (Mal 3:1), the one who would see the beginning of a new age. Still, while there is no greater human being than John, those who commit themselves to Jesus in the coming of the kingdom will have a higher status. It is not that John is excluded but that God is free to give.

Jesus Praises the Father as Revealer, Speaks of Their Mutual Knowledge, and Invites the Audience to Share That Revelation (11:25-30)

In the midst of a section devoted to Jesus' rejection Matthew brings together a group of sayings that underline the revelation that Jesus brings and the kinds of people who accept it. This passage may be divided as follows: (1) the Son praises the Father as revealer (vv 25-26); (2) the Son reveals the mutual knowledge of the Father and himself (v 27); and (3) the Son invites people to share that revelation (vv 28-30).

In the first two verses Jesus concedes, in effect, that the Galilean ministry has not gone well. While the religious experts have rejected his message, the outer fringes of society (IRS, poor, etc.) have accepted it. This was indeed the Father's plan, a plan that did not exclude human malice. In verse 27 Jesus acknowledges that he has a very special relationship with the Father – a relationship that transcends adoptive sonship. The very means for sharing that relationship with others is Jesus himself. Finally in verses 28-30 Jesus offers a share in that unique relationship. Speaking like Lady Wisdom (see Prov 8-9), he invites all who find the Pharisaic law a yoke (see 23:4 – the image is that of an animal harnessed to do work) to accept his own yoke. However, that yoke is bound up with the very person of Jesus – the yoke is Jesus himself, the embodiment of gentleness and humility. To accept Jesus is to attain that final rest that the weekly Sabbath symbolizes

Speech 3: The Parables of the Kingdom (13:1-53)

Jesus Presents the Parable of the Sower, Explains It and Discusses the Purpose of Parables (13:1-23)

This passage marks a new stage in Matthew. Jesus has now met with considerable resistance. This lack of response makes him resort to the veiled language of parables (vv 10-17). Actually the intent of the parables is to teach, to challenge, to confront. Although Matthew has changed the intent of the parables, the parable itself does suggest a point in Jesus' ministry when resistance and lack of response prompted a realistic appraisal of the law of loss and gain in the kingdom. Jesus counters the despair of his ministry by pronouncing this parable of hope.

The parable is really the parable of the seed, not the sower. Apart from verse 3 and the later interpretation in verse 18, the parable deals only with the natural inevitability of success and failure in sowing. (In Palestine sowing often comes before plowing.) There are three states of loss: immediate (path), gradual (rocks), and ultimate (thorns). There are three degrees of gain in the good soil: thirty, sixty, one hundred (hence as diverse as the losses). Significantly the parable spells out how things go wrong (path, rocks, thorns) but not how they go right. The parable thus points to the law of growth and decline in the kingdom. Although one can understand better how things go wrong, one is challenged to hope in that mysterious process whereby they go right. God's mysterious plan is at work: good results do come, although the bad ones are more readily explained.

In verses 10-17 Matthew explains why Jesus speaks to the crowds in parables, i.e., unlike the disciples, they have refused to see and hear his word (contrast Mark 4:11-12). In verses 16-17 Matthew quotes a saying that congratulates the disciples for their seeing and hearing - thus they are the very opposite of those described in the citation from Isaiah 6:9-10 (vv 14-15). In verses 18-23 there is the community's allegorical interpretation of the different dispositions of people toward the proclamation of the kingdom. This probably illustrates the experience of at least some members of Matthew's community.

Jesus Presents Three More Parables and Explains the Parable of the Wheat and the Weeds (13:24-42)

The parable of the wheat and the weeds, i.e., darnel, a poisonous weed, is unique to Matthew. In the first exchange (vv 27-28a) the owner is aware that the weeds represent the work of an enemy. Two problems thus arise: (1) how to save the wheat; and (2) how to outwit the enemy. In the second exchange (vv 28b-30) the owner resolves the two issues. With regard to the first, he will allow both wheat and weeds to grow together until harvest time. With regard to the second, he will use the weeds for fuel. What was originally designed as a disadvantage has now become an advantage.

This parable reflects Jesus' understanding of the kingdom. That kingdom is not an ideal union of only the perfect; it includes, rather, both good and evil. Firm and resolute action is called for, but it is a type of action that recognizes that violence will be counterproductive and that force will endanger the common good. In the kingdom, therefore, both patience and forgiveness are required. The final separation of good and evil is left to the last judgment. Verses 36-43 are probably Matthew's own allegorical interpretation of this parable. Here the Son of Man is the exalted one who presides over the world until the last judgment (see 28:16-20). Jesus' return to the house symbolizes his break with the crowds.

The parables of the mustard seed and the leaven (vv 31-33) make the same basic point, i.e., the contrast between humble beginnings and unexpected endings. Since yeast or leaven symbolized corruption for both Jews and Christians (see 1 Cor 5:6-8), Jesus' use may suggest the outcast sinners he has gathered about himself. Unlike Mark, Matthew adds a formula quotation from Psalm 78:2: Jesus is the wisdom teacher *par excellence.*

Jesus Presents Three More Parables and Describes the Ideal Disciple as a Scribe (13:44-52)

The parables of the buried treasure and the pearl are both unique to Matthew. Both deal with the advent of the kingdom and radical commitment to it: the selling of everything one has. Both have the same sequence: finding, selling, buying. Yet at the same time they are different. In the first parable the farmer is not seeking but happens to find the treasure. In the second the merchant is seeking and finally finds his pearl. In the first there is a certain shock in that the farmer hides the treasure and goes off to buy a seemingly ordinary field. In the second there is less shock since the merchant goes about his purchase quite openly. Quite likely either the tradition or Matthew himself joined the two parables together.

In the treasure parable the first stage is normalcy, namely, the routine work of a farmer whose whole future is plotted out by his circumstances. The second stage is the discovery of the treasure that then creates an entirely new world with new possibilities. The third stage is the reversal of the past whereby the farmer is obliged to sell everything that he has. The fourth stage is the new activity of the farmer made possible by the discovery. He is no longer programmed as before. This fourth stage is the world that Jesus offers the disciples. The kingdom is a world of new possibilities grounded in the person of Jesus.

The parable of the dragnet is also unique to Matthew. It is linked to his explanation of the weeds in 13:36-43 by means of the temporary mixing of good and evil, a final distinction, and appropriate punishment. Matthew stresses that the evil will be rejected and punished.

In verse 52 Jesus describes his disciples by way of a parable. Every scribe trained in the Law and the prophets who also understands his message is like the head of a household. He brings forth from his storeroom both the new (Jesus' message) and the old (the Law and the prophets). For Matthew, such a scribe is the ideal member of his community.

Miracles, Controversies and the Cross (13:52–17:27)

After the Return of the Twelve
Jesus Feeds the Five Thousand (14:13-21)

It is difficult to get back to the original event in the gospel accounts of the feeding of the 5,000 since it is overlaid with tradition and the evangelists' editorial work. There are allusions to the manna in the desert (Exod 16:1-15 - note mention of deserted place), Elisha's feeding of 100 men from 20 barley loaves (2 Kgs 4:42-44 – loaves and fragments), and the Eucharist (26:26 - blessing, breaking, giving). Jesus is viewed as a new Moses and a new messianic king. Like Moses, Jesus provides bread in the desert. Like a messianic king, Jesus hosts a banquet that anticipates the final banquet in the kingdom (26:29).

Jesus' withdrawal (v 13) points to a new period in his ministry, i.e., he withdraws from his enemies until the time of the passion (26:1-2). Once again Matthew emphasizes the compassion of Jesus (see 9:36) that leads him to heal, not teach, as in his source Mark. This compassion also carries over to feeding the crowd. By dropping the disciples' question and Jesus' counterquestion in Mark 6:37-38, Matthew portrays Jesus as totally in charge of the situation. Then, like a Jewish father presiding over the family meal, Jesus blesses, *i.e.*, praises and thanks God for the food. From this point up to 16:12, bread becomes a central image in Matthew. Matthew heightens the effect of the miracle by adding to his source Mark that the 5,000 did not include women and children.

Jesus Walks on the Water (14:22-33)

Matthew adds to Mark's account of Jesus' walking on the waters the tradition about Peter. This is not unlikely Jesus' first postresurrectional appearance to Peter (see John 21:7-8) that Matthew uses to show both divine presence and the believer's dilemma of being caught between faith and doubt.

This scene borrows from the Old Testament: (1) the Lord walks on the waters of chaos (Job 38:16; Isa 43:16); (2) the Lord reaches out to rescue those caught in death's deep waters (Pss 18:16-17; 144:7); (3) the Lord indicates his presence ('It is I') and intent to save (Exod 3:14; Isa 45:18). This tradition implies the following for Matthew's community: (1) when chaos is overwhelming, Jesus is there; (2) when fear overtakes the community, Jesus reacts: 'Do not be afraid' (v 27); and (3) when faith gives way to hesitation, Jesus is willing to stretch out his hand. Unlike his source Mark, Matthew has the disciples reflect the faith of his community. Jesus is not simply another miracle worker – he is the Son of God.

Peter represents the conflict between faith and doubt. 'Little faith' (v 31) captures the dimension of doubt/wavering. Yet Jesus heeds Peter's request by stretching out his hand and the others' request by entering the boat. For Matthew, Jesus does not abandon his community even when the situation appears hopeless. Jesus continues to stretch out his hand and save.

Jesus Accepts the Challenge of the Canaanite Woman (15:21-28)

After having Jesus declare in the preceding episode (15:1-20) that the laws of ritual purity no longer keep Jew and Gentile apart, Matthew now shows Jesus in contact with a Gentile and, indeed, only for the second time. (See the Roman centurion in 8:5-13, a scene that is very close to this one.) Matthew now teaches that the norm for discipleship is not ethnicity but a persistent faith in Jesus, indeed one that overcomes all obstacles. This exceptional case of Jesus and a Gentile woman looks forward to the end of the gospel where Jesus will pronounce the universalism of the community (28:16-20), a reality foreshadowed in the magi account (2:1-12).

It is possible that Matthew intends to keep Jesus within the geographical confines of Israel, hence simply northern Galilee. Verse 22 can mean that the woman came from the district of Tyre and Sidon and, therefore, visits Jesus in Israel. Matthew has changed Mark's 'Syro-Phoenician' into

'Canaanite.' He probably does so to underline the enmity between Jews and Gentiles from the time of the conquest. The woman demonstrates her faith by calling Jesus 'Lord' and 'Son of David' – the Jewish crowds use the latter title in 21:9,15. At first Jesus ignores the woman and the disciples want him to send her away. Having learned the limitations on Jesus' ministry (only to Israel), she challenges Jesus' remark that the Gentiles are nothing but dogs. Not to be outdone, the woman acknowledges Israel's priorities but also insists that some crumbs should fall from the table of Judaism. Because of her overwhelming faith, Jesus bestows some of these crumbs by healing her daughter immediately. By having Jesus accede to her petition, Matthew teaches his community that the criterion for discipleship is this type of unflagging faith.

Peter Confesses Jesus' Messiahship and Becomes the Rock (16:13-20)

In constructing this scene, Matthew uses special material ('M') that probably originated in a postresurrectional appearance of Jesus to Peter (see John 21:15-17; Gal 1:16). Whereas his source Mark has Jesus ask, 'Who do people say that I am?' (8:27) Matthew changes the question to: 'Who do people say that the Son of Man is?' Whereas in Mark Peter identifies Jesus as the Messiah (the Christ), in Matthew Peter adds 'The Son of the living God.' For Matthew, therefore, the Son of Man is not only a son of God as Davidic king, i.e., Messiah (see Ps 2:7), but the transcendent Son of God. Matthew concludes this scene by repeating Mark's command of silence but also by making explicit the title of Messiah (the Christ).

In Matthew Jesus proceeds to reward Peter for his perception, for it is not based on weak human nature ('flesh and blood') but on a revelation received in faith from the Father. Jesus then confers on Peter the grace of leadership. The title 'rock' evokes the unshakeableness he will provide for Jesus' church (see 7:24-27). 'The gates of the netherworld' are the abode of the dead with its insatiable appetite and power. The keys, as seen in Isaiah 22:22, represent the authority of a prime minister and, as seen in 23:13, the power to teach the way to the kingdom. The rabbinic background of binding and loosing implies authoritative teaching and disciplinary power. (See 18:18 where binding/loosing is mentioned within the context of the community.)

At his resurrection Jesus will conquer the gates of the netherworld and dispatch the church on its mission. In that church Peter will be not merely leader of the disciples but the unique foundation that gives solidity to its teaching and authority. Matthew thus combines Christology (the person and mission of Jesus) and ecclesiology (the nature of the Christian community). Peter's awareness of who Jesus is leads to his unique position in Jesus' church.

Jesus Makes His First Passion Prediction and Outlines the Conditions for Discipleship (16:21-27)

This passage is a new subsection of the entire Caesarea Philippi revelation (16:13-28). Here Matthew follows his source Mark with Jesus' first prediction of his passion (v 21) followed by Peter's misunderstanding (vv 22-23) and Jesus' clarification (vv 24-27). As Jesus points out, the route to glory is by way of suffering and death. Jerusalem is significant since it is the city of the martyred prophets. Matthew's mention of Jeremiah as a possible identification of Jesus (16:14) suggests the bond of suffering experienced by both.

Peter cannot accept the implications of Son of Man propounded by Jesus. For Peter, to say Messiah (the Christ)/Son of God is to imply glory and majesty. Jesus, therefore, must reproach Peter since he is an obstacle to God's plans. By acting in this way, Peter plays the role of Satan that Matthew described in the testing scene (4:1-11). Like the devil, Peter opts for the easy manipulative way of buying people off with less than a suffering/death program. As rock, Peter must communicate Jesus' teaching, not purely human plans and programs.

Jesus' fate becomes the disciple's fate. To follow Jesus is to reject the world's security measures. To lose oneself for Jesus is, paradoxically, to find oneself. To gain the whole world but destroy oneself in the process does not turn a profit. But to sacrifice oneself now for Jesus' cause guarantees more than survival on the last day when the glorified Son of Man returns to reward the concrete activities of his disciples.

Jesus Is Transfigured (17:1-9)

Along with the baptism and the agony in the garden, the transfiguration is the key event in which the Father communes with the Son in a special way about his mission. It is likely that the historical kernel of the transfiguration account was a moment of intense prayer for Jesus as he worked through his mission with his Father. Matthew uses the scene to confirm Peter's confession of Jesus as the Messiah (the Christ), the Son of the living God, to anticipate the resurrection, and to establish the link between the Son of the living God and the suffering Son of Man.

The transfiguration is an epiphany, i.e., a manifestation in which a divine figure or figures suddenly and unexpectedly appear and communicate something (in this instance the command to listen to Jesus). Jesus himself becomes such a heavenly figure (note his dazzling white clothes) in the company of Moses and Elijah who already belong to the heavenly realm. According to 2 Kings 2:11 Elijah ascended into heaven in a whirlwind. Though Moses died on Mount Nebo (Deut 34:7), in first-century A.D. tradition he simply disappeared and returned to God. While Moses and Elijah attained heavenly glory without experiencing death, Jesus will experience glory only after enduring suffering and death.

In addition to Jesus' dazzling white clothes, his face also identifies him as a member of the heavenly realm (see 13:43; 28:3). The tent suggests God's dwelling place while the cloud attests God's presence (Exod 40:34-38). The divine voice repeats the proclamation given at the baptism (3:17). Both Moses (Deut 18:15,18) and Elijah (Mal 3:23-24) were expected to fulfill key roles in the coming kingdom. For Matthew, these final days have arrived with the person and mission of Jesus. It is, therefore, only fitting that the Father exhort the audience to listen to Jesus, God's definitive spokesperson (Deut 18:15). Instead of using Mark's 'rabbi,' Matthew has Peter address Jesus as 'Lord.' Fear is a natural reaction to the unfolding of the mystery of Jesus.

Speech 4: Advice to a Divided Community (18:1-35)

Jesus Explains how to Deal with Sinners and Teaches the Efficacy of Common Prayer (18:15-20)

Jesus' fourth great speech in chapter 18 deals with relationships and hence problems within Matthew's community. This passage is a collection of once independent sayings (from 'Q') that Matthew brings together here to bear on the needs of the local church.

Verses 15-17 show the order to be followed in dealing with a sinful member of the community (see Lev 19:17-18; Deut 19:15). The first step is a purely private correction that saves the reputation of the individual. If that fails, a few more witnesses are brought in to prevail upon the sinner. If that is unsuccessful, the admonition of the full assembly of the local community ('the church') is the final step. If the person ignores the full assembly, he is to be excommunicated and regarded as a non-member (Gentile) or a public sinner (tax collector). Verse 18 attests that God ratifies such a decision of the local community.

Verses 19-20 seem to have been originally concerned with the efficacy of common prayer. In their present place they relate to the decision of the local community. Size is insignificant. The presence of merely a few is sufficient to ensure the hearing of the prayer. Christians gathered around the person and words of the Lord are Christ. The risen Lord is present whenever the community gathers (see 1:23; 28:20).

Jesus Teaches the Role of Limitless Forgiveness in the Parable of the Unforgiving Servant (18:21-35)

This passage concludes Matthew's discourse on church order. It is probable that originally the question and answer (vv 21-22 – repeated forgiveness) was separate from the parable (vv 23-34). Quite likely the final verse (v 35) is the work of Matthew himself in order to make the point all the more telling (the threat of punishment against those who refuse to forgive others).

Peter's question is wrong because it seeks to establish limits, although rather generous limits. Jesus' answer (see Gen 4:23-24) refuses to establish any limits at all. Boundless forgiveness is the way of the kingdom.

In the parable the first official owes a boundless debt ('a huge amount' - 10,000 talents). However, his prostration and entreaty move the king to boundless mercy. After all, it was utterly impossible for him to pay the debt. Unfortunately the first official did not experience any change at all. When the second official pleaded in the same position and in practically the same words, the first official showed no mercy, although the debt ('a much smaller amount' - 100 denarii) was payable. The first official finally fell from grace because he refused to share grace. In Matthew's community to be forgiven means to forgive others. However, it cannot be something merely mechanical; it must come from the heart. Such is the way of the kingdom.

Opposition to Jesus (19:1 – 23:39)

Jesus Presents the Parable of the Workers in the Vineyard (20:1-16a)

Jesus' original parable (that is unique to Matthew) seems to be verses 1-13. It may be divided as follows: (1) the hiring of five groups (vv 1-7); and (2) the payment of the groups, beginning with the last (vv 8-13). This unexpected move (v 8) introduces the reversal of expectations described in verses 9-13. It is clear that the landowner has committed no injustice. However, he does appear more as one who offends expectations than as one who is exceptionally generous. On this level the parable teaches that the believer is to accept God's radical freedom, i.e., his ability to give in the face of human calculations and expectations. The believer is to allow God to order the world in God's own way.

Verses 14-16 are probably the work of Matthew himself. In connection with the disciples and their reward in 19:27-30, the parable reminds Matthew's community that Jesus possesses the radical liberty to call and reward others simply on the basis of his generosity (vv 14-15). Leadership positions in the community and outstanding service do not preclude God's freedom to give to others. The 'good' Jesus (19:17) will come back as the Son of Man (19:28) to render judgment as the generous one (v 15). But the judgment will not be based on human calculations.

Jesus Presents the Parable of the Two Sons (21:28-32)

This section (21:23–22:45) takes up Jesus' last controversies with the Jewish leadership, controversies that take place in the temple. This passage is one of three parables on God's judgment of the leadership.

Verses 28-30 may be Jesus' original parable. It may have defended his preaching of the good news to the outcasts, namely, their acceptance by God as opposed to their rejection by the religious establishment. These verses may also exemplify the dichotomy of the believer, i.e., to say one thing but do another. The addition of verses 31-32 creates a new picture. Although these verses do not focus on the saying/not-doing dichotomy, they develop the attitude of the Jewish leaders in 21:23-27. The social outcasts (the tax collectors and the prostitutes) go into the kingdom (vineyard) while the respected leaders do not. The outcasts reacted to the unique manner and message of the Baptist and so repented. The leaders remained recalcitrant and so did not repent. In Matthew's perspective the sayers but non-doers are the Jewish community represented by its leaders; the non-sayers but doers are the Gentiles represented by the social outcasts.

It is significant that repentance is a communal act. It is a reaction to the word of the community's preacher (here John the Baptist) that in turn leads to the community's acceptance into the kingdom. Matthew's community welcomes such outcasts.

Jesus Presents the Parable of the Tenants (21:33-43)

The originl parable of the unjust tenants possibly ended with verse 39. Thus Jesus recounted a disconcerting story of Galilean background. A landowner did not receive his proper share of the harvest from his tenant farmers. Instead, taking advantage of the son's (the third emissary's) status as heir, they killed him.

Christian tradition added the references to the song of the vineyard from Isaiah 5:1-7: the planting of the vineyard (v 33) and the question (v 40). It also interpreted the son as Jesus. But since death was not God's last action on behalf of Jesus, Christian tradition spoke of his exaltation by citing Psalm 118:22-23 (v 42 - see Acts 4:11; 1 Pet 2:7). In the Christian community Jesus' parable of a disconcerting story in Galilee is allegorized as an account of human cruelty offset by divine intervention.

Matthew places this passage as the second of three parables showing Jesus' last controversies with the Jewish leadership (21:23--22:45). In Matthew's hands the parable becomes a judgment on the Jewish leadership. Unlike his source Mark, Matthew speaks of two groups of servants, not two individuals. This may reflect Israel's prophets before and after the exile (see 23:37). However, Jesus is the Father's last spokesperson (note 'finally' in verse 37). Reflecting the historical situation of the crucifixion, Matthew has the tenants drag the son outside the vineyard and only then kill him. Matthew's most important contribution comes in verse 43. After referring to the resurrection (v 42), Matthew has Jesus say that the kingdom will be taken away and given to others. This kingdom will be the church consisting of both Jews and Gentiles. Hence the parable does not pass judgment on the entire people of Israel but only on its leadership. These new tenants will produce the fruit in its proper times.

Jesus Presents the Parable of the Wedding Feast (22:1-14)

Jesus' original parable may have comprised only verses 1-5, 8-10. It may have envisioned a defense of Jesus' practice of eating with sinners. Matthew has enlarged the original setting of an ordinary meal by speaking of a royal wedding feast, a common image of God's final union with his own. Borrowing from the parable of the unjust tenants (21:33-43), Matthew expands the parable in verses 6-7 to create a panorama of salvation history. While seeing the first group of servants as Old Testament prophets (v 3), he probably envisions the second group as Christian missionaries to the Jews (v 4). However, Israel rejects both groups, so that the king is forced to burn their city (probably the destruction of Jerusalem in 70 A.D.). In answer to the question: Who are worthy to share in the final heavenly banquet (v 8), Matthew has the Gentiles brought in from outside. However, it is not a perfect group, consisting as it does, of both good and bad.

Verses 11-13 were originally a separate parable that Matthew now connects with verses 1-10. Not everyone who accepts the call lives up to the implications of the call. The man not properly dressed suffers eternal rejection. Not only Israel but also the Christian community comes under God's judgment.

Verse 14 is an originally separate saying that is calculated to tell members of Matthew's community to take their call seriously. Though the Lord invites many, he chooses only a few. One must continue to respond to the initial call in order to take part in the final banquet.

Jesus deftly Defends Paying Taxes to the Emperor (22:15-21)

The coin of tribute account is part of Jesus' last controversies with the Jewish leadership (21:23–22:45). It is the second controversy story in this section.

The combination of Pharisees and Herodians made for odd bedfellows. The Pharisees rejected the Roman poll tax since it implied Roman domination. The Herodians, supporters of Herod Antipas, accepted the poll tax. Their least common denominator was hostility towards Jesus. By addressing Jesus as teacher, they imply that they are not genuine disciples, since in Matthew this title is reserved for non-believers. Ironically they speak the truth in trying to foil Jesus. Jesus does speak the truth and he abhors human respect (v 16).

Jesus recognizes their bad faith and denounces them as hypocrites. Cleverly, he asks them for the coin. He does not have one; they do. The possession of the coin is the implicit admission of Roman sovereignty. Without trying to distinguish degrees of loyalty, Jesus pronounces the general principle of allegiance to both God and Caesar. If Jesus had refused allegiance to Caesar, he would have been regarded as a revolutionary. If he had simply accepted allegiance to Caesar, he would have been considered disloyal by observant Jews and the popular crowds. In the end the delegation leaves, implicitly acknowledging the ingenuity of Jesus' answer.

Jesus Combines Love of God and Love of Neighbour as the Greatest Commandment (22:34-40)

This passage is also part of Jesus' last controversies with the Jewish leadership. Specifically it is the fourth controversy story of this section.

Unlike his source Mark who presents the issue of the Great Commandment as a friendly scholarly discussion, Matthew views it as a violent attack of the Pharisees on Jesus. Here a lawyer ('a scholar of the law') addresses Jesus with the title 'teacher' - hence the mark of a non-believer in Matthew. Unlike his source Mark who has the scribe applaud Jesus' reply, the lawyer in Matthew sets out to trip Jesus up.

The Great Commandment implies a commandment or commandments that give meaning to all the others. Out of the 248 positive commandments and the 365 prohibitions of the Torah, Jesus selects two: the love of God (Deut 6:5) and the love of neighbor (Lev 19:18). Jesus thus implies that there is a certain order or gradation in the legal corpus. Unlike his source Mark, for Matthew love of neighbor is on a level with love of God. Jesus also adds that these two commandments constitute a basic summary of all the Scriptures ('the whole law and the prophets'). In the end there can be no real love of God without love of neighbor.

For Matthew, Jesus is the very fulfillment of the Law (see 5:17-48). It is the very person of Jesus, not any one commandment as such, that lies at the heart of Christian morality. Nonetheless in 5:17-48 love of neighbor plays a central role (see 5:43).

Jesus Denounces the Scribes and Pharisees (23:1-12)

Chapter 23 in Matthew is the author's condemnation of Pharisaic Judaism. His audience is the crowds, perhaps the despised non-observant Jews (the so-called 'people of the land') and the disciples. The object of the various sayings is the scribes and the Pharisees, namely, the Jewish leadership opposing Matthew's Jewish-Christian community.

By their interpretation of the Law these forces of opposition have created more burdens for the people but have not provided them with any help in bearing them. These forces are also guilty of ostentation: (1) widening the little boxes ('phylacteries') containing passages from the Torah and worn on the forearm and forehead during prayer; (2) lengthening the tassles; (3) seeking out the places of honor at banquets and in synagogues; and (4) longing for marks of respect in public and being hailed as 'rabbi' (literally 'my great one').

Jesus urges avoiding the titles 'rabbi' and 'teacher' since only he is the rabbi and teacher. Secondly, he calls for the avoidance of the title 'Father' since there is only one common father, namely, the heavenly Father (see 6:1). (The title 'Father' was employed for the patriarchs and leading Jewish teachers.) This inveighing against titles suggests that in Matthew's community the notion of service is being neglected. By contrast Matthew proposes the Christian manner of leadership: (1) service (see 20:26); and (2) exaltation/humbling at the final judgment.

Speech 5: The Eschatological Discourse (24:1 – 25:46)

Jesus Urges Vigilance in View of His Return at the End (24:37-44)

Chapters 24-25 constitute Jesus' eschatological discourse or last judgment discourse in Matthew. The first half of this discourse (24:1-36) lines up the order of events leading up to Jesus' second coming. The second half (24:37–25:46) is Matthew's call for vigilance or being prepared. In this passage Matthew provides three parables that are calculated to awaken the Christian sense of watchfulness in view of the Lord's return.

In verses 37-40 Matthew speaks of the flood generation. He warns that they were so preoccupied with their ordinary lives that they neglected to prepare for the great cataclysm. Verses 41-42 then compare two pairs of workers. At the second coming, one worker enters the kingdom while the other does not. Matthew does not pursue the reasons for the choice except to warn that the basis of the choice is vigilance or the lack of it. Finally verses 43-44 depict the modus operandi of the thief, namely, no advance warning but striking at the least likely moment. Here Jesus is the thief (see Rev 3:3). In the end Matthew leaves the reader with something of a paradox. Having enumerated the order of events culminating in the second coming, he next says that the timetable is uncertain. What is certain, however, is the need for vigilance.

Jesus Presents the Parable of the Ten Bridesmaids (23:1-13)

The parable of the bridesmaids (some translate 'virgins' or 'maidens') is one of three parables in this section that deal with the problem of the delay of Jesus' second coming. Besides the delay, Matthew also points out the divisions within the group, the need for prudence, and a permanent state of readiness. Matthew also dismisses every form of frivolity since it does not do justice to the delay.

Although it is difficult to reconstruct the precise wedding customs involved here, it is likely that the bridegroom is returning with his bride from the home of her parents. The bridesmaids are to form part of the joyful procession upon the arrival of the couple. The wise bridesmaids, anticipating the delay, make provisions for such an emergency. However, the foolish bridesmaids demonstrate complete lack of foresight. Once the couple arrives, only the five wise bridesmaids can take part in the procession and thus join in the festivities.

Within the context of Matthew's theology, Jesus is the one who will come at the parousia (second coming), when the wedding banquet, namely, the consummation of the kingdom, will take place. Delay of the second coming, however, should engender watchfulness, not negligence. Not to be prepared is not to be known by the bridegroom. Those who live in the present must still reckon with the future.

Matthew: Speech 5 – The Eschatological Discourse

Jesus Presents the Parable of the Talents (25:14-30)

In this third parable of vigilance Matthew emphasizes responsible behavior in view of Jesus' second coming. He clearly proposes positive action and categorically rules out all fearful or slothful inactivity.

In order to keep his business productive, a weathy businessman entrusts his excess capital to three servants before setting off on a journey. During the time of his absence the servants are to invest the money and increase the master's profits. The first two servants make use of the exorbitant interest rates and so double the original sum. Their fidelity in small matters leads the master upon his return to entrust them with greater matters. Furthermore, they are invited to share the master's intimacy ('share your master's joy'). The third servant, however, refuses to run any risks. He simply buries the sum and unearths it at the master's return. His recital in verses 24-25 paradoxically accentuates the demands of his master.

Given the delay of Jesus' second coming, Matthew insists that the members of his community must behave appropriately. His message is nothing less than an exacting call to positive action.

Jesus Bases Final Judgement on the Recognition or Non-recognition of the Sisters and Brothers of the Son of Man (25:31-46)

In this scene of final judgment Matthew reveals the implications of the vigilance and fidelity mentioned in the parables of chapters 24-25. Vigilance and fidelity are now reduced to recognizing the Son of Man in those whom the world labels of no account: the hungry, the thirsty, the stranger, the naked, the ill, and the imprisoned. The standard or basis of judgment is the recognition or non-recognition of those sisters and brothers of the Son of Man.

Jesus appears in all the trappings of regal splendor. As king, he sits upon the royal throne. He also exercises his kingship by his role as shepherd. Just as a shepherd separates sheep from goats at night, so the Son of Man separates the blessed from the condemned. Fittingly the sheep enjoy the place of honor on the right while the goats are placed on the left.

In the dialogue with the two groups what emerges is a christological criterion. The Son of Man - the king/shepherd - identifies with all those who suffer. Within the context of the judgment the 'least ones' are all those who experience any form of need. The christological criterion thereby becomes ecumenical.

The Passion, Death and Resurrection of Jesus (26:14 – 28:20)

Matthew Recounts Jesus' Passion and Death (26:14–27:66)

While Matthew's passion account depends in part on Mark, Matthew has adapted Mark and introduced his own material. Principal emphases in Matthew include the following: (1) Jesus' willing acceptance of the passion as God's plan for him; (2) the connection of that plan with the fulfillment of Scripture; and (3) Jesus' sovereign authority.

For Matthew, Jesus is the obedient Son of God who faithfully does God's will to the point of death in fulfillment of the Scriptures. In commissioning his disciples to prepare the Passover meal, he remarks: "My appointed time draws near" (26:18). In the garden, while his disciples sleep, he continues to pray that his Father's will, not his own, be done (26:36-46). Jesus thus expresses in his very person God's intended will for his people.

Jesus' death on the cross concludes his redemptive mission and thereby frees God's people from sin and death. At the Last Supper he identifies the cup as his blood of the covenant that will effect forgiveness of sins (26:28). The cosmic signs at his death (splitting of rocks, quaking of the earth, opening of tombs - 27:51-53) announce his victory over death. As his name 'Jesus' indicates, 'he will save his people from their sins' (1:21). His powerful ministry of teaching and healing symbolizes his victory over death in its myriad forms.

Jesus is the Son of Man whose humiliating death achieves final victory. At the Jewish trial he informs the high priest Caiaphas that the Son of Man will be seated at God's right hand and will come on the clouds of heaven (26:64). In the passion narrative the Sanhedrin (26:67-68), the Roman cohort (27:27-32), and those present on Golgotha (27:38-44) mock Jesus but nonetheless God's power becomes manifest in Jesus' weakness.

In his suffering Jesus demonstrates the deepest meaning of righteousness. He is the exemplar of genuine faith. As he experiences the absence of God on the cross (27:46), the lament prayer of Psalm 22 lingers on his lips. He will not separate himself from his Father or his Father's will. Faith in the midst of horrific anguish defines his sense of righteousness.

After the Angel's Appearance to the Women Jesus Meets Them and Directs Them to Announce His Resurrection (28:1-10)

This passage contains two scenes: (1) the tomb event (vv 1-8); and (2) Jesus' appearance to the women (vv 9-10). It should be noted that none of the New Testament traditions describes the actual resurrection experience of Jesus since there were no witnesses to this scene. This accounts, in part, for the differences in the traditions. Thus Matthew, while making use of Mark, departs significantly. Whereas in Mark the women go to the tomb to anoint Jesus, in Matthew they come to inspect the tomb. In Matthew there is no discussion of rolling back the stone since it is not applicable. Unlike Mark, Matthew mentions the guards at the tomb to connect them with the burial tradition (27:62-66). In Mark the women are bewildered when they leave the tomb; in Matthew they are both frightened and elated.

In the first scene Matthew has reduced Mark's three women to two to connect with the women who witnessed the tomb (27:61). At the approach of the women there is an earthquake that reminds the reader of the earthquake at the death of Jesus (27:51-54). The earthquake as well as the apparel of the angel (see Dan 7:9; Rev 1:14-16) smack of apocalyptic imagery. They announce the shaking of the world's foundations at Jesus' conquest of death. The posture of the angel, i.e., sitting on the stone, also dramatizes Jesus' victory. The impact on the guards (v 4) is a contrast to 27:54. At the cross the guards witness the earthquake and become believers. At the tomb the guards witness the earthquake but do not become believers. Typical of a theophany (divine manifestation) is the opening phrase: 'Do not be afraid' (v 10). The angel's message is to proclaim that the crucified one is now the risen one, hence a vindication of Jesus' own prediction (16:21; 17:23). Although the angel invites the women to examine the tomb, he quickly urges them to announce the good news. The women thereby become the first heralds of the resurrection. With a mixture of joy and fear, the women leave to seek out the as yet unbelieving male disciples.

Although verses 9-10 are unique to Matthew, there are parallels with John 20:14-18. Jesus' greeting leads to an act of homage and reverence. Although Jesus' message seems to repeat the words of the angel, there are significant emphases to suggest it is not mere repetition. Thus the body of Jesus is a real body. Moreover, by using the expression 'my brothers' (v 10), Jesus communicates forgiveness to the sinful disciples. Finally the purpose of Jesus is not to renew old friendships but to initiate the mission of the Church (Galilee).

Jesus Commissions the Eleven and Assures Them of His Abiding Presence (28:16-20)

In this passage Matthew has no departure of Jesus (hence no mention of the ascension). Verse 18b announces the fact of his exaltation, i.e., the granting of full authority over the entire universe. The accent, rather, is on Jesus' abiding presence. This final scene in the gospel is the commissioning of the Eleven. Its format may come from the commissioning of a prophet (see Exodus 3:7-17; 4:1-16). After introducing the scene, Matthew has the Eleven confront Jesus and react by both worshiping and doubting. Jesus then confirms the Eleven, assuring them that he has full authority. Next he commissions them to go, make disciples, and baptize. Finally he assures them of his abiding presence.

In this scene the disciples enter into an intimate relationship with Jesus. Like the Old Testament prophets, they have become members of God's council (see Isa 40:1-11). Thus they share in his deliberations and are privy to his resolutions. They are to communicate their experience of God's action in Jesus to the whole world by baptizing and making disciples of all nations (hence the Gentiles). In the face of temptations and doubts, they have Jesus' assurance that he will remain with them always (see 'Emmanuel' or 'God with us' in 1:23).

Concluding Reflections on the Gospel of Matthew

Some fifty to sixty years after the death and resurrection of Jesus, as the Jerusalem temple lay in ruins, the author of Matthew addresses the state of the Jewish people. He asks: Where can a Jew find a faithful interpretation of the Torah? Rejecting emerging rabbinic Judaism, this author urges his audience to look to the life and message of Jesus the Teacher. He presents this Jesus as the fulfillment of Israel's Scriptures. His genealogy reveals that he is rooted in the history of his people. Like Moses, he experiences the sojourn in Egypt but returns to his native land to assume his mission of teaching.

To emphasizes Jesus as the Teacher of Israel, the author of Matthew constructs five great speeches. In the Sermon on the Mount Jesus deepens the understanding of the Scriptures. Assuming the posture of a teacher (sitting - 5:1), he assures his audience that he has come, not to abolish the Torah and the prophets but to fulfill them (5:17). Unlike Moses on Mount Sinai, Jesus does not receive God's revelation - rather, he gives it. Sensing that he will need assistance in sharing this revelation, he offers his missionary discourse. His disciples will share his mission, one involving rejection. However, if the missionaries lose their life for Jesus' sake, they will find it (10:39). In his third speech he explains in parables the profound meaning of the kingdom of heaven. The parables of the mustard seed and leaven contrast the humble beginnings and unexpected endings of this kingdom (13:31-32). In his discourse to a divided community Jesus insists that his community is not a perfect society and hence must exhibit patience and forgiveness (18:21-35). Finally in his fifth speech Jesus presents the last judgment as a collage of disguises. His disciples must discover his presence among the marginalized (25:31-46).

In addressing his Jewish-Christian audience, the author of Matthew seeks to win over not only non-Christian Jews but also the Gentiles. To this end he recounts the story of the magi who are led to the newborn king of the Jews by a star (2:2) while both Herod the Great and the Jewish leadership reject him. In the scene of the great commissioning (28:19) he announces to the Eleven that they are to make disciples of all nations. Although Jesus the Jew views his teaching ministry as confined to Israel (10:5-6; 15:24), he nonetheless heals the Roman centurion's servant (8:5-13) and the Canaanite woman's daughter (15:21-28).

The Jesus of Matthew is not an absentee teacher. Rather, he continues to abide with his Church. In the infancy narrative he receives the name 'Emmanuel' that the author interprets as 'God is with us' (1:23). This name assumes added significance when the exalted Jesus makes this solemn pledge: "And behold, I am with you always, until the end of the age" (28:20). Even when catastrophe strikes and Matthew's community experiences great danger, Jesus will be as near as he was during the violent storm on the lake. His comforting message will be the same: "Take courage, it is I; do not be afraid" (14:27). Moreover, even if only two or three gather for prayer in his name, he will be in their very midst (18:20).

Finally this Jesus of Matthew encourages a special intimacy with his disciples whom he calls the salt of the earth and the light of the world (5:13-14). As teacher, he shares with them the mutual knowledge of his Father and himself (11:27). As a cautious teacher, he recognizes that they are often overworked and heavily burdened. In such circumstances he urges them to learn from him who is meek and humble of heart (11:29). The Jesus of Matthew remains the Teacher right up to the very end.

The Jesus of Luke

The Setting of the Gospel of Luke

Unlike the other evangelists, Luke narrates not only the ministry of Jesus culminating in his death and resurrection but also a sequel entitled the Acts of the Apostles. In this sequel Luke traces the growth and development of the Christian message from Palestine into Asia Minor and Europe, concluding with Paul's house arrest in Rome, the heart of the Roman Empire. With this outreach he connects the events of the early church to those of Jesus' ministry.

In the gospel Luke follows Mark's tripartite divison: Galilean ministry, journey to Jerusalem, and Jerusalem ministry. However, Luke is most concerned to move Jesus without distraction from Galilee to Jerusalem. To achieve this, he omits Mark 6:45–8:26 with their mention of Jesus' excursions to Bethsaida, Tyre, Sidon, and the Decapolis (sometimes called Luke's 'Great Omission'). Jesus' journey to the city of destiny is so paramount that Luke expands Mark's journey of two and a half chapters into 10 (9:51–19:27). In terms of discipleship Luke thus exhorts the believer to follow Jesus resolutely on this journey. As he remarks in 9:57, the disciples 'were proceeding on their journey ... '

Luke is also intent on anchoring his gospel account in time and human history. Thus he places the announcement of John the Baptist's birth 'in the days of Herod, King of Judea' (1:5). He also provides a time line for the start of the Baptist's ministry by mentioning the Emperor Tiberius, the Roman prefect Pontius Pilate, and the high priests Annas and Caiaphas (3:1-2). Similarly, he situates the birth of Jesus during the reign of the Emperor Augustus and the governorship of Quirinius (2:1-2). For Luke, therefore, the story about Jesus and the church is public knowledge and incontestable (see Acts 26:26).

Like Matthew, Luke probably writes between 80 and 90 A.D., perhaps in Greece. However, there is no convincing evidence that Luke used Matthew or *vice versa*. In addition to Mark, Luke also uses 'Q' and his own special source ('L'). The author of this gospel is generally thought to be a Gentile-Christian of the second generation (see 1:2) who addresses a mainly Gentile-Christian audience. He endeavors to help this audience in their own self-understanding. He assures these Christians that their acceptance of Jesus is part of God's plan that reaches back to creation. The gospel message they have received rests on those 'who were eyewitnesses from the beginning and ministers of the word' (1:2).

The Jesus of Luke is the Prophet. A prophet is not essentially one who predicts the future but a spokesperson for God. At times a prophet must speak God's condemning word, pointing out the audience's sinfulness and need for reform (criticizing function). At other times a prophet must articulate a message of hope, indicating how things can be different (energizing function). For example, in 21:5-6 Jesus must announce the destruction of the temple. In 4:18 he proclaims that his mission is to bring glad tidings to the poor and announce liberty to the captives. As God's prophet, Jesus must always insist on his Father's viewpoint concerning the world and people.

Luke Introduces His Gospel with a Formal Prologue (1:1-4)

Unlike Mark and Matthew, Luke provides a formal prologue to his gospel (see Acts 1:1-2 for the appropriate prologue to his second volume). Here Luke informs his readers that he has employed both oral and written sources. He also appears to pride himself on his personal and accurate research. In other words he has used his sources critically. Seemingly dissatisfied with earlier efforts by others, he intends to write 'in an orderly sequence' (v 3). Addressing fellow Christians, he assures them of his purpose to provide certainty, not surmise, about both past and present events. Luke dedicates this work to Theophilus (meaning 'friend or lover of God'), a Gentile-Christian who is most likely not only his patron but also the one financially responsible for sponsoring the publications.

Luke has determined to extend the biblical narrative and show how the Gentile-Christian community of his own day enjoys continuity with a loyal and renewed Israel. To achieve this goal, he will characterize Jesus as the Prophet who has come to restore his people.

Infancy Narratives (1:26 — 2:52)

Luke Narrates the Angel Gabriel's Annunciation to Mary (1:26-38)

In his infancy narrative Luke invites the reader into the world of the Old Testament. Here temple, Torah, and canticles hold center stage. Luke seems to be reminding his readership that the origins of both Jesus and the Church are rooted in the history of Israel.

Luke's account of the annunciation to Mary is not a blow-by-blow account of God's actual communication to Mary but a theological picture of the significance of Jesus drawn from Old Testament models. In keeping with the annunciation literary genre in the birth narratives of Ishmael, Isaac, and others, there is an appearance of an angel (v 26) that leads to the recipient's fear (vv 29-30). In verses 31-33 there follows the message itself, with the description of Jesus as the Davidic Messiah (vv 32-33 – see 2 Samuel 7:8-14). This in turn provokes Mary's question in verse 34, *i.e.*, the apparent impossibility of compliance because of her virginal status. The question thus articulates Luke's description of the Davidic Messiah in verse 35, namely, Son of God through God's creative Spirit. Finally, a sign is given to confirm God's intent, namely, Elizabeth's conception (v 36), although Mary does not ask for a sign.

Here Luke has opted to contrast Mary with Zechariah, the father of John the Baptist, in the preceding annuciation (1:5-25). There Zechariah asks for a sign and is punished for his lack of faith. Mary, however, is totally open to God's plan, identifying herself as 'the handmaid of the Lord' (v 38). This depiction of Mary derives from her role during Jesus' ministry and thereafter. According to 8:19-21; 11:27-28 she is one of Jesus' disciples. Indeed, for Luke she is the model disciple because she hears God's word and acts upon it. In Acts 1:14 Luke presents her as part of the prayerful Pentecost community. For Luke, Mary's openness to God's word begins at the conception of Jesus.

Mary Visits Elizabeth (1:39-45)

For Luke, the Visitation is a command from God. In 1:36-37 the angel gave as a sign Elizabeth's miraculous pregnancy. In 1:38 Mary expressed her obedience by identifying herself as the handmaid of the Lord. Her haste in going into the hill country reflects this obedience to God's plan. The Visitation fulfills the sign given.

The Baptist begins his prophetic mission right from the womb (see 1:15). He causes his mother to recognize the Messiah in Mary's womb, just as he would later help others to recognize the one mightier than he (3:16) and so prepare the way of the Lord (3:4). Elizabeth's canticle (vv 42-45) reminds the reader of Deborah who praised Jael as 'most blessed of women' (Judges 5:24) for her part in God's salvific plan. 'Blessed is the fruit of your womb' is a blessing promised by Moses for obedience to the covenant (see Deuteronomy 28:4).

Elizabeth's canticle is linked to the New Testament too (see 11:27-28 that is unique to Luke). Mary's privilege is not a purely personal one; she has a decisive part to play in God's plan. Elizabeth's praise, 'Blessed is the fruit of your womb,' matches that of the woman in the crowd, 'Blessed is the womb that carried you and the breasts at which you nursed' (11:27). However, Elizabeth's beatitude, 'Blessed are you who believed,' corresponds to Jesus' reaction to the woman in the crowd, 'Rather, blessed are those who hear the word of God and observe it' (11:28). In Luke's view Mary is the great believer, *i.e.*, she brings to God's plan a deep faith, a faith that acknowledges that the Lord's plan will be fulfilled. Agains Luke offers the faith response of Mary as a contrast to the unbelieving Zechariah (see 1:18,20).

Mary Sings Her Canticle (1:46-45)

Quite likely verse 56 followed immediately after verses 39-45 (the Visitation). Luke apparently wanted to feature only the parents and the newborn in his birth narratives of Jesus and the Baptist. Hence he has Mary leave Elizabeth prior to the birth of the Baptist. At a later point he probably inserted the *Magnificat* as Mary's response to Elizabeth's canticle (vv 42-45).

The *Magnificat* is probably a non-Lucan composition of God's saving action in general that Luke appropriated for his infancy narrative. The piety of this canticle (from the circles of those called *anawim, i.e.*, the poor ones totally reliant on God for support) corresponds to the piety of Mary in the narrative. The setting is now the conception of Jesus reflecting the hymn of Hannah in 1 Samuel 2:1-10. The introduction (vv 46b-47) expresses Mary's joy. Verses 48-50 provide motives for praising God, *e.g.*, the overcoming of her lowliness (Mary's virginity is tantamount to the barrenness of the Old Testament matriarchs) and the Exodus-like accomplishments ('great things' – see Deuteronomy 10:21). Verses 51-52 anticipate the victory to be achieved through Jesus' passion and resurrection, *i.e.*, the time when God's arm will be manifested and Jesus will be exalted to God's right hand (see Acts 2:33). Verse 53 continues God's reversal strategy ('hungry ... rich'). Finally, God proves true to his covenantal promises by providing help (see the covenant with Abraham in verse 55).

Jesus Is Born in Bethlehem (2:1-14)

Taken as a whole, 2:1-20 has the following structure: (1) setting including the census (vv 1-5) and the birth/swaddling (vv 6-7); (2) annunciation including the angel's message/sign (vv 8-12) and the appearance of the heavenly host reciting the *Gloria* (vv 13-14); (3) reactions including the shepherds' visit to Bethlehem (vv 15-17) and the effect on Mary and the other hearers (vv 18-20). For Luke, the significant element is the angel's message, not the birth, since the message interprets the event for the shepherds.

Historically, Quirinius, while legate in Syria, had only one census in 6-7 A.D. and this affected Judea, not Galilee (see also Luke's confusion in Acts 5:37). Luke, therefore, moves Mary and Joseph from Nazareth to Bethlehem for his own purposes. Augustus provides the appropriate setting since Jesus will be saviour of all those registered. Augustus was also hailed as saviour of the whole world. However, for Luke, that real peace came only from Jesus. Hence the heavenly host announces peace 'to those on whom his favour rests.'

The manger may refer to Isaiah 1:3 where the Greek text says that an ass knows its master's manger. The inn may have in mind Jeremiah 14:8 where only the passing traveler spends the night whereas Jesus is permanently present. The swaddling may allude to Wisdom 7:4-5 in which the great King Solomon is swaddled. Luke pictures Jesus as born in the city of David, *i.e.*, Bethlehem (although Jerusalem, according to 2 Samuel 5:7,9, is the city of David). Furthermore, Luke presents him as born in a manger where God's people now recognize their Lord, not in the lodging of a night traveler who is merely passing through. Finally, Luke suggests Jesus' regal dignity by the use of swaddling clothes.

Luke introduces the shepherds because of their association with Bethlehem (see 'Tower of the Flock' [Gen 35:19-21; Mic 4:8; 5:1]). Using a text such as Isaiah 9:5, Luke has the shepherds announce that a Messiah (Christ), son of David, has been born who is Savior and Lord. The reality of the exaltation is already present in the conception and birth of Jesus. There next follows a theophany or divine manifestation ('the heavenly host'). The angels thus recognize in the beginning what the disciples will recognize in the end, namely, their Messiah (Christ).

The Shepherds Visit Jesus in Bethlehem (2:15-20)

This passage is part of the larger structure of the birth of Jesus (2:1-20 – see above). This third part (vv 15 -20) deals with reactions including the shepherds' visit to Bethlehem (vv 15-17) and the effect on Mary and the rest of the audience (vv 18-20).

In verse 15 the shepherds decide to verify the message of the angel. The baby lying in the manger probably alludes to Isaiah 1:3. Israel finally recognizes the manger of its Lord, the place where God provides for his people. Here Luke adds two reactions: (1) that of the shepherds themselves; and (2) that of the audience ('All who heard it'). The shepherds react by understanding the angel's message about the child. When they subsequently return, they break out into praise of God. They thereby anticipate those generations of believers who will also glorify the Lord for what they have heard and seen. The audience reacts by being astonished. Yet among all the astonished in this infancy narrative (see 1:63), only Mary is described as keeping and reflecting on these events.

Mary's reaction (v 19) is more telling for Luke since Mary is the only witness in the infancy narrative who reappears in the ministry of Jesus. The Greek verb translated 'reflecting' refers to the God-given interpretation of hidden events. As Luke's model disciple, Mary will correctly interpret these events only after Jesus' exaltation. For the present, however, she must still ponder the mystery of her child.

After the Shepherds' Visit Jesus Is Circumcised (2:16-21)

When the shepherds have completed their mission, they leave, glorifying and praising God. They are the first believers in Jesus. Luke notes that the recipients of the shepherds' report were amazed (v 18). However, he does not observe that these recipients actually reflected on them in their hearts. By contrast, it is Mary who anxiously keeps all these things, reflecting on them in her heart (v 19). She is thus presented as pondering the God-given interpretation of these obscure happenings. For Luke, this is significant since Mary is the only one in the infancy narrative who will be the link with Jesus' later ministry. Mary, therefore, is set apart as the one who reflects in faith on the mystery yet to be revealed. Luke appropriately regards her as a believer and disciple (see 1:38; 8:19-21; 11:27-28; Acts 1:14).

In contrast to the Baptist's circumcision and naming (1:59), Jesus' circumcision and naming are rather parenthetical. Instead of discussing the legal significance of the circumcision, Luke connects the naming to 1:31. Naming the child 'Jesus' fulfills the angel's command.

Jesus Is Presented in the Temple (2:22-40)

This passage may be divided as follows: (1) parents' presentation of the child in the temple (vv 22-24); (2) Simeon's greeting and twofold oracle (vv 25-35); (3) Anna's greeting (vv 36-38); and (4) conclusion (vv 39-40). The Old Testament background for Simeon and Anna is the figures of Eli and Hannah in 1 Samuel 1-2. Luke also seems to have the text of Malachi 3:1-2 in mind: 'And the LORD whom you seek will come suddenly to his temple ... But who can endure the day of his coming?'

Although only the purification (see Leviticus 12:1-8) required going to the sanctuary, Luke mentions the offering of the firstborn male (see Exodus 13:2,12,15) since this leads to the meeting with Simeon, the Eli who confronts the latter-day Elkanah and Hannah, *i.e.*, Joseph and Mary. Luke indicates the greatness of Jesus by dwelling on the law of the Lord (vv 22-24,27,39), the prophetic Spirit (vv 25-27), and the temple cult. In the *Nunc Dimittis* (that borrows from Second Isaiah) Luke anticipates the Acts of the Apostles, *i.e.*, that the Gentiles are also God's people (Acts 15:14; 28:28).

In the second oracle (vv 34-35) Luke has Simeon anticipate (1) the Jewish rejection of Jesus during the ministry and the passion and (2) the Christian overture to Israel in Acts. In the process of discrimination (the sword) Mary will experience pain as Israel as a whole fails to respond.

In Anna the prophetess (together with Simeon) Luke probably has in mind the gift of the Spirit at Pentecost. Anna represents the devout (*anawim*) of Israel – not unlike Judith 8:5-6. In verse 40 ('filled with wisdom … and the favour of God was upon him') Luke probably alludes to 1 Samuel 2:21,26, namely, Samuel's development. The reader is thus prepared when Jesus appears in the Nazareth synagogue (4:22).

Jesus Is Lost and then Found in the Temple (2:41-52)

This passage is a transitional story from the presentation in the temple (2:22-40) to the beginning of the public ministry (3:1). Its purpose is christological in that it foreshadows and anticipates the mystery that will culminate in the exaltation. Stories of this type are at home in other literatures. There too they allow the reader to glimpse the greatness of the person at an early age. Luke has built this account around the saying in verse 49 that provokes the failure to understand the revelation in verse 50.

Luke mentions for the first time the going up from Nazareth or Galilee to Jerusalem. However, this anticipates the journey in the ministry of Jesus that will bring him to Jerusalem at Passover (9:51–19:27). The listening and the asking of questions look to the future when Jesus will openly engage in such debate, although the atmosphere is peaceful here. The astonishment of the parents has in view the astonishment at the start of Jesus' ministry (4:32) and the amazement of the scribes at his answers. Jesus' reply to his parents indicates that his first allegiance is to his Father's will, not his family's feelings. 'In my Father's house' (v 49) identifies Jesus as God's Son.

In verses 51-52 Luke tones down somewhat the sharpness of verse 49. He presents Jesus as a model of piety who observed the fourth commandment and only exceptionally answered his parents back. He also depicts Mary as open to the mystery of her Son. 'Keeping all these things in her heart' (v 51) provides a place for Mary as a member of the community (see Acts 1:14). Mary thus symbolizes the postresurrectional Christian community. She too was searching for a better expression of what she had sensed all along. This scene in the temple shows that her Son's question called for a change in her. Acts 1:14 reveals that she was prepared for that change.

Preparation for Jesus' Public Ministry
(3:1 — 4:13)

John the Baptist Proclaims a Baptism of Repentance (3:1-6)

Following Mark's order in this section, Luke emphasizes the central role of the Baptist. His ministry is the beginning of the good news that prepares for the ministry of Jesus (see Acts 1:21-22). At the same time Luke does not hesitate to distinguish the roles of John and Jesus. Again following Mark, Luke relegates John's position to that of precursor.

Luke begins the ministry of John the Baptist with a highly formal chronology, naming both the civil and religious rulers. Although there are problems, a likely date is towards the end of the year 27 A.D. This chronology implies Luke's concern to register these events as part of world history. Luke's outlook is clearly universal, seeing the the coming of Jesus as affecting Gentiles as well as Jews.

Unlike Mark and Matthew, Luke emphasizes to a greater degree the differences between the Baptist and Jesus. He limits John's sphere of activity to 'the whole region of the Jordan' (v 3), omitting the fact that all the Judean countryside and the people of Jerusalem went to the Baptist in large numbers (Mark 1:5). Luke also omits the description of the Baptist as Elijah and even the fact of Jesus' baptism by John (Mark 1:6,9). In Luke, John does not say that one mightier than he is coming after him (Mark 1:7), simply that one mightier than he is coming (v 16). For Luke, the Baptist is the greatest and last prophet of Israel but with Jesus a completely new period beings (16:16; Acts 13:24-25).

Following Mark, Luke cites Isaiah 40 and thus understands John as pointing out a new and definitive second Exodus. What is significant is that Luke, unlike his source Mark, prolongs the citation to include Isaiah 40:4, namely, that all humankind (flesh) shall see the salvation of God (v 6). This further testifies to the universal scope of Luke's two-volume work.

John Preaches to the Crowds and Announces the Coming of a Mightier One (3:10-18)

Verses 10-14 are unique to Luke. Here the Baptist offers advice to the crowds, the tax collectors, and finally the soldiers. The tax collectors were known to use extortion in order to make a profit (they first had to pay the Roman government for this right). The soldiers may be the tax collectors' bodyguards who would 'shake the people down' in order to get the taxes from them. For such hated classes, Luke had a message of redemption.

The Baptist's ministry had given rise to the hope that he might be the

Messiah. Luke dismisses this possibility with the Baptist's statement (v 16). To add to the vast difference between John and Jesus, Luke omits the phrase 'after me' in: 'one mightier than I is coming.' The spheres of John and Jesus must be kept distinct.

At this point Luke offers another contrast. John is a fiery eschatological preacher of divine judgment: spirit, fire, winnowing fan (see Numbers 31:23; Isaiah 29:5-6; Malachi 3:2-3,19). Jesus' approach, however, will be decidedly different. As Jesus will announce in the synagogue sermon (4:18-19), it will be a programme of mercy. As demonstrated in Jesus' reply to John's two disciples (7:22-23), it will be a programme that will scandalize the Baptist. John's preaching of the good news is significant but still inadequate. With Jesus a new age will dawn.

Jesus Is Baptised (3:15-16,22)

Messianic agitation surrounds the work of the Baptist in Luke. Phrases such as 'filled with expectation' and 'all were asking in their hearts' (v 15) build up an atmosphere of messianic expectation (see 7:19-20). The Baptist resolves the question by contrasting his person and work with those of Jesus. Luke thus reacts to certain groups that tried to exalt the Baptist at the expense of Jesus (see John 1:8,20). John baptizes in water whereas Jesus will baptize 'with the Holy Spirit and fire' (v 16). In its original use, such a phrase referred to the fiery, violent inbreaking of God's judgment (see Isaiah 30:27-28; 66:15), although Luke can use it in a Christian sense (see Acts 1:5; 11:16).

The baptism of Jesus is a historical fact (its very mention implies some sort of embarrassment). For Luke, it is Jesus' intimate experience and vision of God in relation to his mission. Luke, however, adapts the event to his own theological needs. He connects the baptism of Jesus with the baptism of all the people. He does not say that John baptized Jesus. Instead, Luke subordinates the baptisms to Jesus' prayer, a very important element in Luke's theology (see 5:16; 6:12; 9:18). From the very start of the ministry, Luke portrays Jesus as preparing for the arrival of the new messianic kingdom and the making of a new people of God. This is the solemn inauguration of Jesus' mission.

Luke stresses the prophetic aspect of Jesus' mission. The opening of the heavens makes the descent of the Spirit possible. The Old Testament background is Isaiah 63:19 where God is asked to 'rend the heavens and come down.' After a long period of silence God now speaks. In Isaiah 63:10-11,14 the spirit is linked to the making of a new people. The dove may symbolize Israel, especially coming out of exile and returning home (see Psalm 68:14; Hosea 11:11). The voice from heaven is a revelation or divine communication that quotes Isaiah 42:1. Jesus is thus assured of his status as beloved Son ('servant' in the Hebrew text). The voice emphasizes that, like the Servant of Isaiah, Jesus will have a prophetic mission. This passage also adds: 'Upon him I have put my spirit.'

Jesus Is Tempted in the Desert (4:1-13)

Luke begins his account of the temptation by noting that Jesus 'was led by the Spirit into the desert' (v 1). This is a clear link with the baptism of Jesus and hence his prophetic mission. A confrontation is beginning to emerge between the Spirit and the devil. Luke has also changed the order of the temptations (from 'Q'), making Matthew's third temptation ('a very high mountain') his second ('took him up'). Here Jesus has an interior vision ('in a single instant') of the devil's kingdom and power. As used elsewhere in Luke, 'power' means political power (see 7:8; 12:11). The devil, therefore, enjoys political power. As a result, there will be a conflict between Jesus' kingdom and the devil's kingdom. In Luke's theology, Jerusalem (named specifically in the third temptation) is significant as the place where his gospel begins and the place from which the good news will penetrate to the ends of the earth. In this instance, Jerusalem prefigures Jesus' passion. It will be at the time of the passion that the devil will have his next opportunity ('he departed from him for a time' - see 22:3,53). Apart from that, Jesus' victory over the devil is definitive.

Luke found Jesus' replies in his source 'Q' - all three come from Deuteronomy (8:3; 6:13,16) and refer to Israel's temptation in the desert. Unlike the old Israel, Jesus, the new Israel, endures. Jesus, therefore, is faithful to his Father. He will continue to be faithful to the mission confided to him at his baptism. As this passage demonstrates, Jesus cannot be bought, cajoled, or manipulated by the ruler of this world.

Jesus' Galilean Ministry
(4:14 — 9:50)

Jesus Begins His Galilean Ministry
and Preaches in the Nazareth Synagogue (4:14-21)

Luke begins Jesus' Galilean ministry with his inaugural address in the Nazareth synagogue. Unlike his source Mark, Luke does not immediately state the content of Jesus' preaching (see Mark 1:15). That will come only in the course of this synagogue address. Moreover, Luke places the rejection of Jesus at the beginning of his ministry, not later (contrast Mark 6:1-6). On the positive side, this Nazareth scene introduces Jesus' Galilean ministry (4:14–9:50) and anticipates the great fame attached to his preaching. After his baptism, Jesus returned from the Jordan 'filled with the Holy Spirit' (4:1). Luke continues that Spirit theology here. After his temptation in the desert, Jesus returns to Galilee 'in the power of the Spirit' (v 14).

In the synagogue Jesus stands for the reading but sits for the sermon. He chooses the text of Isaiah 61:1-2, but Luke omits the phrase 'to bind up the brokenhearted' and substitutes Isaiah 58:6, *i.e.*, 'letting the oppressed go free'. Luke does not have Jesus cite the end of Isaiah 61:2, *i.e.*, 'a day of vindication', because it does not fit the scope of Jesus' preaching. Jesus' anointing is a prophetic anointing that is connected with his baptism (3:22). His prophetic message is to bring good news ('glad tidings') to the poor and to announce the jubilee year (see Leviticus 25:8-55), *i.e.*, the time when all debts are cancelled and all property restored to the original owners. Jesus the Prophet states that the text of Isaiah has been fulfilled through his Spirit-filled presence.

Jesus Is Rejected by His Nazareth Townspeople (4:21-30)

This conclusion of the synagogue service in Luke anticipates the incredulity of the Jews and the mission to the Gentiles. Jesus announces a new age by applying the texts of Isaiah to himself. The synagogue sermon is, in effect, his inaugural address.

The first reaction is amazement. The people are astonished that a simple man like Jesus can actually proclaim the fulfillment of such a great message. In turn, Jesus reacts by presenting himself as a prophet rejected by the hometown people. He then illustrates the universalist thrust of his mission by citing the miracles of Elijah (1 Kings 17:7-24) and Elisha (2 Kings 5:1-27) – in fact, Luke is the only evangelist who mentions these miracles. Their relevance is that they benefited Gentiles. The good news rejected by the Jews will be preached to the Gentiles (see Acts 13:46-50).

The original admiration of the audience now turns to indignation. Jesus' hour has not yet arrived (see 4:13); hence he simply 'passes through the midst of them' (v 30). As used elsewhere, the verb 'to pass through' or 'walk/go' implies Jesus' ultimate trek to death and ultimately to glory. Thus the Spirit-filled proclaimer of the new era must go down the path that leads through hostility and pain to exoneration. This whole scene is truly programmatic.

Jesus Calls His First Disciples (5:1-11)

In this passage Luke has used his sources to dramatize the implications of

Peter's call. Unlike Mark 1:16-18, Luke first has Jesus preach from Peter's boat. He then adds the miraculous catch of fish that in turn provokes Peter's reaction. At first, Peter addresses Jesus as 'Master' (v 5), but after the catch he appeals to him as 'Lord' (v 8). Peter now realizes that he is in the presence of one sent by God. He is constrained to ask Jesus to leave because his own sinfulness clashes with the holiness of God's envoy. At this point Jesus addresses only Peter (contrast Mark 1:17). He offers Peter a lifelong career as a unique fisherman in God's employ.

This passage is probably a post-resurrectional story of the first appearance of Jesus to Peter (the account has much in common with John 21:1-14). This would account for: (1) the use of 'Lord' (v 8); (2) the commission to catch humans (verse 10 corresponds to the fishing scene in John 21); and (3) the command not to be afraid that is typical of postresurrectional appearances (see Matthew 28:10; Luke 24:37-38).

The conclusion of this account is important for Luke's theology. In both Mark 1:20 and Matthew 4:20 the disciples leave their nets and Zebedee. In Luke, however, the disciples leave everything. It is, therefore, a question of radical renunciation and hence total dedication. Later (in Luke 18:28) Peter will state: "We have given up our possessions and followed you' (see also Acts 4:32-35). Luke's message is the following: be detached from your possessions and place yourselves at the service of your neighbour.

Jesus Begins His Sermon on the Plain (6:17,20-26)

Verse 17 is the beginning of Luke's Sermon on the Plain (6:17-49) that is comparable to Matthew's Sermon on the Mount. Unlike Matthew who uses 'Blessed are the poor...', Luke employs the second person: 'Blessed are you who are poor...'. 'Kingdom' (v 20) evokes the image of the ideal ancient Near Eastern king who provides especially for the disenfranchised (the poor, the afflicted, the lowly – see Psalm 72:4,12-14). Here in Luke, Jesus appears as both wise man ('blessed') and prophet ('woe'). 'Blessed' in the Old Testament (see Psalm 1:1) possesses a notion of envy or desirableness. Hence Jesus states that the situation of the poor, the hungry, the sorrowing, and the persecuted is enviable because of God's involvement. 'Woe' was initially a call to funeral mourning (see 1 Kings 13:30; Jeremiah 22:18) that the prophets adapted. In their hands 'woe' expressed the disaster that would come upon various classes of Israel's society because of violations of the covenant (see Isaiah 5:8-25).

The first three beatitudes (vv 20-21) reflect the joy of Jesus' early ministry. By announcing the enviable lot of the poor, the hungry, and the sorrowing, Jesus proclaims that the messianic kingdom has arrived in his very person. These people are enviable because Jesus claims for himself the

Davidic prerogative of providing for them. On the other hand, the fourth beatitude (v 22) reflects the hostility of Jesus' enemies, coming towards the end of his ministry. Thus the lot of those followers who share in the prophetic fate of Jesus is now declared enviable.

Luke himself is probably the author of the four woes (note the abrupt change between vv 26 and 27). They reveal the situation in Luke's community that is composed in large measure of the poor. These woes change the meaning of the beatitudes. The lot of the poor, the hungry, and the sorrowful is enviable because they do not exist only for the present world and their condition will ultimately be reversed. At the same time the woes are a powerful appeal to the wealthy and the powerful to meet the needs of the poor and the weak.

Jesus Continues His Sermon on the Plain (6:27-38)

Although Luke used the same source ('Q') from which Matthew also derived his Sermon on the Mount material, Luke offers a wider outlook and tends to separate Jesus' teaching from its Jewish matrix. For example, where Matthew speaks about tax collectors (5:46) and pagans (5:47), Luke omits these references and speaks about sinners in general (vv 32-34). Moreover, Luke seems more bent upon describing actions that express the Christian spirit than upon describing that spirit as such.

In verses 27-38 Luke offers three sets of ideal norms: (1) verses 27-31; (2) verses 32-36; and (3) verses 37-38. In the first set Luke mentions love of enemies (vv 27-28), non-retaliation (v 29), and generosity without recompense (v 30). In verse 31 Luke provides the motivation: 'Do to others as you would have them do to you.' In the second set Luke lists loving (v 32), doing good (v 33), and lending (v 34). In verses 35-36 he supplies the motivation, namely, love of enemies and imitation of the compassionate Father. In the third set Luke has: not judging / not condemning (v 37a), forgiving (v 37b), and giving / good measure (v 38a). In verse 38b Luke inserts the motivation: 'For the measure with which you measure will in return be measured out to you.'

Luke presents these norms as the basic Christian attitudes. They are basically Christian wisdom, *i.e.*, they are attitudes expressive of those who are called 'blessed.' As Christian wisdom, they also look to concrete application. It is interesting to note how Luke can employ both 'human' (v 31) and 'divine' principles (v 36).

Jesus Continues His Sermon on the Plain (6:39-45)

In his Sermon on the Plain, Luke offers not only norms (6:27-38) but also parabolic sayings (6:30-45) and a final parable (6:46-49). In verses 39-40 Jesus warns against becoming self-righteous, *i.e.*, attempting to improve others while ignoring one's own obvious weaknesses. The real disciple is to be concerned about professionalism. He or she should absorb Jesus' teaching and then transmit it accurately.

Verses 39-40 prepare for verses 41-42. The proverbial saying about the splinter and the beam is a colourful way of saying that moral improvement begins at home. Only after one's own house is in order, should one venture forth to correct others. Correction of others implies previous self-correction. The opposite is hypocrisy.

Verses 43-45 enlarge the preceding. The results tell everything. Thus there is a correspondence between a person's character and actions. For a good person whose will ('heart') is bent upon concern for God and fellow humans, goodness will result. On the other hand, from an evil person whose will ('heart') is bent upon pursuit of self, only evil will result. The will ('heart') is ultimately the determining factor.

Jesus Heals the Centurion's Servant (7:1-10)

Luke uses the story of the cure of the centurion's servant to illustrate the faith response expressed at the close of his discourse in 6:47-49. Luke also employs the story to elaborate continuity between Israel and the Gentile world. Where Matthew has the centurion directly petitioning Jesus (see Matthew 8:5), Luke uses Jewish elders who then mention the centurion's kindnesses towards Israel.

In telling the story Luke emphasizes two points: (1) the cure of the slave without personal contact; and (2) recognition of the power of Jesus' word. The centurion, therefore, sends a second delegation that stresses his unworthiness. Although Jesus does not hesitate to enter a Gentile's house, the centurion is nonetheless aware of the Jewish sensitivities involved. Against the background of Roman military discipline the centurion acknowledges the authority of Jesus' word. To give a command is to see it executed. At this point Jesus must recognize the faith of the centurion that outstrips the faith Jesus has experiencd among his Jewish people. The statement of the cure (v 10) attests to the power mentioned above.

Jesus Raises the Son of the Widow of Nain (7:11-17)

In the raising of the widow's son Luke borrows from an Elijah miracle story (see 1 Kings 17:17-24). He uses this account to show that Jesus is truly a prophet (v 16). More important, perhaps, is that while Jesus is an Elijah-figure, he does not bring about the end time associated with Elijah.

Luke: Jesus' Galilean Ministry

For Luke, there is no imminent second coming (*parousia*).

Since the dead man was the widow's only son, her existence was most precarious since, like the woman in 1 Kings 17:17-24, she had no breadwinner. Verse 13 underlines Jesus' great compassion. Here Luke has Jesus called 'Lord' – the title later applied by the Christian community to Jesus in view of his resurrection. The conqueror of death now finds himself in the presence of death. Just as Jesus did not hesitate to enter the centurion's house (7:6), here he does not shrink from touching the coffin and thus becoming ritually unclean. Whereas Elijah prayed three times to the Lord (1 Kings 17:21), Jesus speaks on his own authority. By restoring life to the son, Jesus restores life to the widow – she can now survive in this male-dominated society. In verse 16 the crowd reacts to the miracle: 'A great prophet has arisen in our midst' and 'God has visited his people.' 'A great prophet' may be linked to the popular expectation of Elijah's return.

Jesus Forgives the Sinful Woman and Counts Women among his Closest Followers (7:36–8:3)

Luke's story of the anointing varies significantly from the accounts of the other evangelists (see Matthew 26:6-13; Mark 14:3-9; John 12:1-8). What emerges with total clarity is Jesus' understanding of the kingdom. It is nothing less than the refuge of sinners. It is not the aggregate of a few righteous.

The contrast between Jesus and Simon is stark. Simon recognizes Jesus as a rabbi, perhaps as a prophet. He forgoes the outward signs of a warm Near Eastern welcome. He then sits in judgment on both Jesus and the woman. The woman in Simon's judgment is obviously a sinner and, therefore, to be avoided. Jesus, however, welcomes her demonstrations of affection and, therefore, cannot be a prophet. Simon has clearly set limits to the forgiveness of sins. On the other hand, Jesus recognizes that, though the woman' reputation remains, her life has entirely changed. He consequently welcomes the affection lavished by the woman since her faith has prompted her sorrow. To make the point clear to Simon, Jesus relates the parable wherein gratitude to the forgiver is in proportion to the sins forgiven. The woman is forgiven much, as is obvious from the fact that she has loved much. For Jesus, the kingdom means setting no limitations to God's ability and willingness to forgive. Jesus and Simon differ because their understandings of the kingdom differ.

In 8:1-3 Luke has Jesus continue to break down barriers associated with a false understanding of the kingdom. In 7:36-50 the barrier was the sinfulness of the woman. In 8:1-3 the barrier is women in general. Rejecting the usual rabbinical practice of not having women disciples, here Jesus associates women with the Twelve. At the same time Luke is also preparing for the women's roles of witness in the passion and resurrection accounts (see 23:49,55; 24:10,22-23). Some of the women, *e.g.*, Joanna, were women of means. It is hardly by accident, therefore, that Luke later speaks of the role played by prominent women in the early Church (see Acts 17:4).

Jesus Feeds the Five Thousand (9:11b-17)

Luke places this multiplication scene at the climax of Jesus' Galilean ministry where it figures as part of his plan for the kingdom. In Jewish literature such a banquet scene is very familiar. According to Isaiah 25:6-8 the Lord will wipe away the reproach and anxiety of his people and provide a great banquet. More specifically, 2 Kings 4:42-44 supplies a background in which Elijah provides for 100 men from 20 barley loaves. In the gospel tradition the account is a miracle story, although there is no mention of the multiplication of the loaves by Jesus. The miracle appears only with the mention of the 12 baskets. The miracle is secondary, the sense of solidarity is primary.

Like his source Mark, Luke has highlighted the Eucharistic dimension of the multiplication. Here, at the Last Supper, and on the road to Emmaus, Luke mentions the same actions: taking, blessing / thanking, breaking, giving (see 22:29; 24:30). The bread is a sign of their solidarity with Jesus. On other occasions (13:29; 14:15) Jesus speaks of the kingdom in terms of a meal. To break bread with Jesus means to belong to his kingdom.

After Peter's Confession, Jesus Makes His First Passion Prediction (9:18-24)

Peter's confession is one of the key events in the gospel tradition. Luke's mention of Jesus at prayer (v 18) enhances its significance. The event presupposes that Jesus has been pondering his destiny, that he has come to realize that only his death and resurrection will usher in the kingdom. The replies of the disciples suggest that he has not discussed his messiahship publicly and, therefore, the general public has not picked up any real clues as to his messianic identity.

Jesus acknowledges Peter's perception but goes beyond it. Jesus is here pictured as resolving the question of his identity by using three titles. The Messiah (Christ) was the anointed Davidic king pledged especially to provide for the poor and disenfranchised. However, the title took on some connotations of power that Jesus would judge unacceptable. Jesus, therefore, combines Messiah (Christ) with Son of Man and Suffering Servant. In Daniel 7 and the pre-Christian Book of Enoch, the Son of Man is a divine being hidden in God's presence who would be revealed in the end to preside in glory over God's kingdom. According to Isaiah 52:13–53:12 the Suffering Servant degrades himself as a guilt-offering but he is finally exonerated for effecting the survival of the nation. Jesus, therefore, will be Messiah (Christ), but only as Suffering Son of Man.

In verse 23 Luke has Jesus address everyone, not only his disciples. The essence of following Jesus is to forget oneself and daily (Luke's addition to Mark) carry one's cross. This means the following paradox: if you win, you lose; but if you lose, you win.

Jesus Is Transfigured (9:28b-36)

The transfiguration captures a crisis in the life of Jesus. Luke links the account with the preceding scene (9:18-24) where Jesus reveals his passion, death, and resurrection. The voice from the cloud looks back to his baptism (3:22) and hence his prophetic mission. The overshadowing (v 34) suggests the work of the Spirit at his conception (1:35). At the same time the transfiguration prefigures the ascension. The cloud, the two heavenly witnesses, the dazzling white clothes, and the mountain suggest the ascension at the beginning of Acts (1:6-12). There on the Mount of Olives a cloud lifts Jesus up and two men dressed in white appear.

The transfiguration is an epiphany, i.e., a manifestation in which a divine figure or figures suddenly and unexpectedly appear and communicate something (in this instance the command to listen to Jesus). Jesus himself becomes such a heavenly figure (note his dazzling white clothes) in the company of Moses and Elijah who already belong to the heavenly realm. According to 2 Kings 2:11 Elijah ascended into heaven in a whirlwind. Though Moses died on Mount Nebo (Deuteronomy 34:7), in first-century A.D. tradition he simply disappeared and returned to God. While Moses and Elijah attained heavenly glory without experiencing death, Jesus will experience glory only after enduring suffering and death.

Moses and Elijah traditionally represent the Law and the prophets respectively. Moreover, they too experienced crises but also the assurance of God's presence and support on the mountain (see Exodus 34:29 for Moses' radiant face and 1 Kings 19:11-13 for Elijah). Here they discuss Jesus' *exodos*, a term that includes the passion, death, and resurrection. In this experience of the heavenly world (note Jesus' tent and God's Tent of Meeting in Exodus 40:35), Jesus is assured that his forthcoming passion and death will not be the end. It is a step in the Father's plan whereby the cross is the condition for the glory of the resurrection/ascension (24:26).

Jesus' Journey to Jerusalem
(9:51 — 19:27)

Jesus Begins His Journey to Jerusalem
and Sets Conditions for Discipleship (9:51-62)

This passage is the beginning of Luke's Travel Document. The 'being taken up' (v 51) refers to the entire complex of passion / death/ resurrection / ascension. At this point (Jesus' 'days were fulfilled') Jesus initiates this complex by heading for Jerusalem. He sets his face like flint ('resolutely determined'). This indicates Jesus' prophetic determination to attain his objective (see Isaiah 50:7; Jeremiah 21:10; Ezekiel 6:2).

The Samaritan episode (vv 52-56) – the only episode in the Synoptics (Matthew, Mark, and Luke) that takes place in Samaria – is significant for Luke's Gentile mission. Luke implies that this mission already begins during Jesus' lifetime. At this point, however, the Samaritans cannot accept Jesus. This non-acceptance stems from Jesus' Jewish ancestry and perhaps also from reluctance to accept the prophetic fate associated with Jerusalem, namely, his death. In turn, the non-acceptance gives way to misunderstandings on the part of James and John. Their desire to wipe out the Samaritans indicates that they have not yet accepted a suffering Messiah.

Verses 57-62 contain three sayings of Jesus concerning discipleship. It is significant that Jesus teaches the rigours of discipleship 'as they were proceeding on their journey' (v 57). Thus the disciple is invited to join Jesus on his trek to Jerusalem. Discipleship, however, is no easy matter. The Son of Man who has nowhere to lay his head (v 58) appeals to the highest of motives. Jesus' saying in verse 60 about letting the dead bury the dead means wholehearted commitment that allows no delay. The third requirement (v 61) resembles Elisha's plea in 1 Kings 19:20. Unlike Elijah, Jesus permits no turning back (note the ploughing scene in 1 Kings 19:19).

Jesus Sends the Seventy-two on Mission
and Welcomes Them on Their Return (10:1-12,17-20)

Towards the end of the first century A.D. Luke's community was largely Gentile. In this passage Luke anticipates the thrust of Acts, namely, the proclamation of the good news to the Gentiles. Although Luke shares with his source Mark the mission of the Twelve (see Mark 6:7-13), Luke alone has the mission of the Seventy-two. The reading can be either 'seventy' or 'seventy-two'. It is likely that the number symbolizes the 70 nations in Genesis 10 (or 72 according to the Greek Bible). Luke thus establishes continuity for the missionaries of his own time. They too have a mandate

Luke: Jesus' Journey to Jerusalem

from Jesus and thus participate in his mission.

There is a great sense of urgency in this charge – the harvest does not last long. The missionaries must forego the barest necessities, even omitting the common courtesies of Near Eastern wayside conduct (see 2 Kings 4:29). The opposition ('the wolves') will attempt to minimize their efforts. Yet God will provide for them in such crises. Moreover, in keeping with the Gentile community, the missionaries need not fret over non-kosher foods.

Their message is that the kingdom has arrived. 'Kingdom' suggests the task of the ancient Near Eastern king in meeting the needs of his people, especially the disenfranchised (see Psalm 72:12-14). Hence in Jesus and his missionaries God is present to people and their needs. Indeed Luke proposes different forms of that presence: word of mouth communication of the good news, healing of the sick, and bestowal of peace. With regard to rejection of their message, the missionaries are not to act like James and John in Samaria (9:54). They are to use the prophetic symbol of repudiation (see 9:5; Acts 13:51). By shaking the dust from their feet, they declare themselves free of the fate that follows upon rejection of the word. Sodom – a biblical synonym for depravity – will have it easier on the day of judgment.

Upon their return the missionaries reveal their great delight. To their remarks about the demons Jesus replies that they did counteract Satan's influence (see Revelation 12:9). In verse 19 Jesus adds that he has put his own power into their hands. However, the basis of this jubilation should not be the ability to contain the demons but to retain their proper relationship to God (Revelation 20:12).

Jesus Presents the Parable of the Good Samaritan (10:25-37)

According to Mark 12:28-31 in response to the question about the Great Commandment Jesus combined Deuteronomy 6:5 (love of God) and Leviticus 19:18 (love of neighbour). In this passage from Luke it is a scholar of the law who offers the same combination. Besides focusing on inheriting eternal life, Luke goes another route by exploring the word 'neighbour'. Aware of the categories of people included in the term, Luke makes his parable hinge on the scholar's question ('And who is my neighbour?'). This question implies a larger question, namely, who can belong to God's covenant community? The answer (v 37) indicates that anyone who observes the command of mercy belongs to God's community.

To establish his point, Luke makes the hero of the parable a Samaritan, a non-Jew and hence one excluded from the category of neighbour. The villains of the piece are the priest and the Levite. By touching a corpse, a priest would become ritually unclean and, depending on circumstances, so would the Levite. For these two Jews the meticulous observance of the purity laws takes precedence over love of neighbour (presumably the traveller was a fellow Jew). By showing compassion, the Samaritan can become a member of God's community. In Luke's community there is room for everyone – Jew, Samaritan, or Gentile – provided one accepts this definition of neighbour: my neighbour is anyone who needs my help.

Jesus Visits Martha and Mary (10:38-42)

Of all the evangelists Luke displays the greatest interest in women. He sees them against a larger background of human dignity and liberation. In 8:1-3 women play a key role in the ministry of Jesus and in Acts 18 Priscilla assists in the foundation of a Christian community and in convert-instruction.

In this passage Martha welcomes Jesus, the divine visitor (note the title 'Lord'), as a guest. Luke's intention is not to disparage Martha and her household chores. Rather, his intention is to show that discipleship pre-empts all other concerns. In a world where women did not receive *Torah* instruction from a rabbi, Luke relates that Jesus and Mary function as teacher and disciple. Mary's posture (sitting) and the insistence on the words of Jesus suggest religious instruction. 'There is need of only one thing' (v 42) implies that the basic reality of hospitality is to focus on the guest and consider everything else secondary or optional. By her attentiveness Mary has acknowledged the presence of the Prophet since a prophet is defined by his word.

Jesus Delivers the Our Father
and Gives Further Instructions on Prayer (11:1-13)

In Luke's Hellenistic world all prayer is impersonal and prayer of petition is of doubtful value. To his predominantly Gentile-Christian audience Luke proposes Jesus as the model of prayer. It is significant that Jesus himself is at prayer prior to instructing the disciples. The disciples thus experience God as Father because they share Jesus' experience of God as Father. 'Father' bears a deeply intimate sense. As a result, the disciples are drawn into the family circle.

As opposed to Matthew (Matthew 6:11), Luke asks for daily bread each day (not today). To exemplify this petition, Luke offers the parable of the unexpected guest (unique to Luke). Although the relationship is that of friends, the lesson of persevering prayer is clear. The bond of friendship and the virtue of perseverance ultimately win out.

In verses 9-13 Luke returns to the father-son relationship. If human fathers so provide for their sons, with all the more reason will the Father provide for his children. Instead of giving 'good things' (Matthew 7:11), the Father gives the Holy Spirit. Luke is probably envisioning persecuted Christians who need strength to withstand their ordeal (see 12:11-12). The caring Father appreciates the predicaments of his family.

Jesus Inveighs against Greed and Presents the Parable of the Rich Fool (12:13-21)

The opening verses of this passage (vv 13-15) provide the occasion for Luke's parable of the rich fool. Although recognized as an authority by the people, Jesus refuses to render a legal judgment – he is not the proper arbiter. Moreover, the question is wrong. Jesus points out to the crowd that possessions do not of themselves make for living in the kingdom.

In the parable Jesus describes a man who completely fails to read the situation and act appropriately. The words 'life' and 'fool' capture the thrust of the parable. Life connotes the entire person – here, the rich man with his personal identity in contrast to possessions. At the same time life includes an existence that transcends this life. In his pursuit of self, the rich man confuses his total self with his body. Against the background of the wisdom literature (see Job 2:10; 30:8), the farmer has violated healthy community life. By envisioning everything solely in the context of his desires, he demonstrates the lack of wisdom needed for true human development. He is a fool, a colossal failure.

Verse 21 interprets the parable. The quest of the rich man is an ego trip. It is a matter solely of himself – his wealth and his lifestyle. This verse states categorically that to grow wealthy only for oneself is to court judgment and death. Wealth by its very nature requires concern for others.

Jesus Encourages the Giving of Alms and in a Parable Contrasts Faithful and Unfaithful Servants (12:32-48)

Luke derives this passage from 'Q' (see Matthew 6:19-21; 24:43-51) but the differences between Matthew and Luke are significant. Only Luke (v 32) assures his persecuted community that they are Jesus' flock and that hence he will care for them. While Matthew 6:10 speaks of 'not storing up treasures on earth.' Luke is more positive: 'Sell your belongings and give alms' (v 33).

Luke's exhortation to be vigilant in view of the master's return is similar to Matthew's parable about the ten bridesmaids / virgins (Matthew 25:1-13). However, Luke emphasizes how the master waits on his faithful servants and meets their needs.

In the parable contrasting the faithful and unfaithful servants (vv 39-46 – see Matthew 24:43-51), Luke introduces two significant changes from Matthew. In verse 42 he changes 'servant' to 'steward.' Luke also has Peter introduce the parable by asking about its applicability (v 41). To be sure, such changes are hardly accidental. While all Christians are bound to be faithful, it is especially the stewards or leaders, symbolized by Peter, who have the greater responsibility. They are not to use their power to abuse the members of the community. Their power implies communal service, not personal gain.

The concluding section (vv 47-48) is unique to Luke. Gifts imply responsibility. The greater the gift, the greater the responsibility.

Jesus Becomes a Cause of Divisions (12:49-53)

Luke presents Jesus in this passage as focusing on decision-making. He describes his mission in terms of fire. He has come to separate the true from the false, using fire as a purifying agent (see Malachi 3:4). His fire will necessarily provoke a decision: in one case, acceptance of his person and message; in another, rejection of his person and message. Jesus' own death goes hand in hand with the fire imagery. For the third time (see 9:22,44) he speaks about his passion. Water symbolizes anguish and frustration (Psalms 40:3; 69:2), and baptism relates to his death (see Mark 10:38-39). Jesus, however, cannot hold back his desire for the 'baptism' to take place since it will release the Spirit and complete the purifying process (see Acts 15:9-10).

As anticipated in Simeon's prophecy (2:34-35), Jesus' message will result in division, a decision for or against God. Jesus' person and message will divide households. Here both Matthew (10:35-36) and Luke (v 53) rely on the prophet Micah's (7:6) description of family turmoil. Whereas Matthew has only the contempt of the younger generation for the older, Luke makes both generations responsible but places the older first. The person and message of Jesus must provoke a decision.

Jesus Proclaims Universal Repentance and Presents the Parable of the Fig Tree (13:1-9)

This passage that is found only in Luke is part of a larger section devoted to the theme of vigilance and readiness (see, *e.g.*, 12:54-59). This account is composed of two parts. The first part (vv 1-5) stresses the need for universal repentance. The second part (vv 6-9), the parable of the fig tree, emphasizes the possibility of mercy for those who repent in time.

There is some historical basis for the reference to Pilate's treatment of

Luke: Jesus' Journey to Jerusalem

the Galileans. In any event, Jesus does not accept the view that the fate of the Galileans equals their guilt. To bolster his argument, Jesus cites the example of the 18 killed at Siloam. What does emerge, however, is the constant need to reform. Similarly, the parable of the fig tree shows that repentance must occur now, for tomorrow may be too late. For Luke's community, the words of Jesus point out the implications of their Christian call. They have to be ever alert and hence ever willing to renew their original Christian commitment in following Jesus.

Jesus Underlines the Role of Fidelity in the Quest for Salvation (13:22-30)

Only fidelity gets one into the kingdom. Luke sounds this ominous note by connecting this scene with Jesus' journey to Jerusalem (v 22) that will result in the inauguration of the kingdom. Jesus dismisses the bystander's question about the number of those to be saved. It is simply the wrong question. The right question is: How does one get into the kingdom? Jesus' answer is in the plural ('He answered them') – hence a message for Luke's wider audience. In reply, Luke brings together two originally separate sayings of Jesus about doors. The narrow door (v 24) means personal responsibility – religious status is meaningless. The closed door (vv 25-27) suggests personal fidelity – personal relationship is useless. Though the kingdom-seekers properly address the master as 'Lord', they will still find themselves outside. Evildoers (see Ps 6:6) have not reacted properly to Jesus' prophetic word (6:47).

These 'all-talk, no-show' people will catch a glimpse of the residents of God's kingdom (vv 28-29). They will see the following guests: patriarchs, prophets, but also the outsiders, namely, the Gentiles. To become a guest, one must heed God's word. Finally (v 30) Jesus tells his audience that seating in the kingdom depends on fidelity, not rank. Luke's audience should learn from Israel's mistake.

Jesus Dines with a Pharisee and Offers Instructions for Proper Banquet Etiquette (14:1,7-14)

In this passage Luke has taken sayings of Jesus from different occasions (vv 2-6,7-11,12-14,15-24) and placed them in one meal setting. They all answer the question: Who can eat bread in God's kingdom?

In verse 1 Luke informs his readership that this is a festive Sabbath meal given by a leading Pharisee and one to which religious leaders would naturally be invited. The scramble for places at the dais provokes Jesus' saying about humbling and exaltation (v 11) and offers a first response to the question posed above. In the kingdom there is room only for those who can perceive the value of others and accept it joyfully.

In verses 12-14 Luke connects the previous self-flaunting with the guest-list arrangement. In human relationships people tend to view others not as people but as objects. Hence it is a question of inviting only those who can reciprocate at a later date. The guest list thereby becomes a cryptic form of IOUs. In answer to the question, Jesus now replies that one who treats people without a view to a reward here and now can eat bread in God's kingdom. One must expect a reward outside history at a point that only faith can perceive. For Luke's audience, living in a world of 'favours returned for favours given,' Jesus' saying about inviting the poor, the lame, etc. must have had no little impact. Faith without expectation of a reward now is the lifestyle of the kingdom.

Jesus Offers Advice on Discipleship (14:25-33)

In this passage Luke addresses this question: How high is the price of discipleship? The opening verse suggests the enlisting of recruits, but the enlisting is set against the background of the trek to Jerusalem. In response to this question, Luke has combined three sayings (vv 26-27,33) and two parables (vv 28-32), inserting the parables between the second and third sayings.

'To hate' means that Jesus must be so uppermost in the lives of his disciples that one's family appears to be despised (Matthew 10:37 expresses this notion as 'to love more'). Taking up one's cross after Jesus binds the follower to the experience of the passion (see 23:26 where Simon of Cyrene carries the cross behind Jesus). Allegiance to Jesus must be so total that possessions are not permitted to lessen that bond in any way. However, it is not the unconditional demand to renounce all property (see Acts 5:4-5). But neither is it exaggeration for the sake of emphasis.

The two parables comment on weighing the cost of discipleship. Both the tower builder and the warring king demonstrate that the follower must calculate the costs, investigate the risks, and estimate the overall demands of discipleship. The price of discipleship is high indeed.

Jesus Vindicates the Right not to Limit God's Goodness, in Three Parables (15:1-32)

The introduction of this passage (vv 1-3) shows that in Luke's community some were demanding stringent requirements for sinners. In this series of parables Luke does not have Jesus proclaim the good news. Rather, he has Jesus vindicate the right not to put limits on God's goodness.

In the parables of the lost sheep and the lost coin the shepherd and the woman, respectively, seem to be worried over what is relatively insignificant: one sheep out of 100 and one coin out of ten. But the Pharisees and the scribes are guilty of precisely that – they have perverted values. They are more concerned about paltry things than about people, namely, sinners. If the finding of one sheep and one coin provokes joy, all the more so the finding of lost humans. To join in the celebration means to join in the recovery of lost values.

The parable of the prodigal son has two dimensions: the return of the younger son (vv 11-24) and the protest of the older son (vv 25-32). Both sections end with the same saying: 'dead … come to life again … lost … found.' In the first section the embrace and the kiss are the signs of forgiveness. Moreover, the father's orders to his servants (vv 22-23) reinforce the forgiveness. To be feasted is to be welcomed home. On the other hand, the older son refuses to join in the festivities. He refers to his younger brother as 'your son' (v 30); in contrast the father calls the older brother 'my son' (v 31) and the younger son 'your brother' (v 32). For Luke, the father and the younger son reveal what God is like while the older son reveals what his critics are like. The reader is still left wondering if the older son will stay outside pouting or join the party rejoicing.

Jesus Presents the Parable of the Dishonest Stewart and Applies It (16:1-13)

This passage consists of the parable of the dishonest steward (vv 1-9) and some originally isolated sayings of Jesus (vv 10-13) that further interpret the proper use of wealth for the disciples.

In the parable Luke uses the enterprising steward as a model of prudence. When faced with the prospect of losing his position, he begins to juggle the books. In order to ingratiate himself with his master's debtors, he 'generously' invites them to change the figures on the original contracts. Learning of the steward's machinations, the master is forced to applaud his ingenuity. In turn, the steward becomes the model for disciples. God's people ('the children of light') should display as much prudence in dealing with God and their destiny as the worldly ('the children of this world') display in their areas of concern. Proper use of wealth is part of a disciple's calling. Finally the disciples are exhorted to use 'dishonest wealth' justly so that they may be welcomed into the lasting abode of the righteous.

Verses 10-11 correct the impression of the parable by making honest use of the criterion for judging. Verse 12 points out that the faithless use of another's goods endangers one's true destiny. Finally verse 13 inveighs against all compromise.

Jesus Presents the Parable of the Rich Man and Lazarus (16:19-31)

In this parable that is unique to him, Luke develops the theme of the exaltation of the poor and the humbling of the rich (see 1:52-53), alluding as well to his beatitudes and woes in the Sermon on the Plain (6:20-21,24-25). He also appears to address the parable to the Pharisees (16:15) who were in danger of interpreting wealth as a sign of righteousness.

Significantly, Luke gives the beggar a proper name. (Lazarus is Greek for Eleazar, meaning 'God helps or has helped'.) On the other hand, the rich man has no real identity because he has chosen to isolate himself from others in his world of non-concern. While the rich man has 'proper company,' Lazarus has only the dogs. Death, however, reveals Lazarus as a person and the rich man as a nonentity – wealth and security are obviously no guarantee of God's favour. Even in the netherworld the rich man remains in character. He orders Abraham to order Lazarus to perform services for him. At this juncture such communication is impossible. After all, the rich man had erected this chasm while he was yet living.

The conclusion of the parable is a violent reaction to Jesus' audience that demands signs as proof. Luke seems to imply that, although the apostles preached the resurrection of Jesus by appealing to Moses and the prophets, the response of Israel as a whole was paltry. To receive the Scriptures that witness to Jesus, one must first be open in faith. In turn, this presupposes that one senses a need. Lazarus perceived such a need, but the rich man did not.

Jesus Emphasises the Essential Role of Faith (17:5-10)

This passage consists of a centerpiece of faith (vv 5-6) around which Luke gathers originally separate sayings relative to faith: verses 1-2 on offence, verses 3-4 on forgiveness, verses 7-10 on putting the master in the slave's debt.

In response to the apostles' request, Jesus notes that it is not a question of more or less faith but of faith pure and simple. He teaches this by way of illustration, *i.e.*, telling a tree to be uprooted and transplanted in the sea. Whereas Luke's source Mark (11:23) speaks of a mountain and associates Jesus' saying with the cursing of a fig tree, Luke employs a tree and inserts the simile of the mustard seed (see Matthew 17:20). The Greek text speaks of a sycamine, not a sycamore, tree. The sycamine or black mulberry has an elaborate system of roots. Hence with a faith as small yet as dynamic as a mustard seed, one could uproot the sycamine and transplant it in a more unusual habitat, namely, the sea.

In verses 7-10 Jesus speaks about servants, *i.e.*, church leaders who should employ faith in fulfilling the tasks expected of them. In preaching the good news, such leaders should not seek out rewards – they are supposed to preach the good news (see 1 Corinthians 9:16). Although Luke often describes God as Father, leaders should recognize that special consideration is something freely given in view of special performance only.

Jesus Cleanses the Ten Lepers (17:11-19)

In this account of the ten lepers Luke relates the fundamental misunderstanding of Israel. In the section immediately preceding (17:7-10), the leader is taught to perform his office without seeking rewards. In this leper story the nine Jews look upon their cure as something owed them by God. It is only the Samaritan who recognizes God's great generosity. Thus a Samaritan (hence a foreigner) becomes a model for Israel and an example of God's overture to the Gentiles. It is Luke who sees the cure of Naaman in Jesus' inaugural address (4:27) as symbolic of God's openness to the Gentiles.

Unlike Naaman (see 2 Kings 5), the ten lepers were so afflicted that they had to keep their proper distance. In responding to their request, Jesus does not heal them immediately but merely tells them to carry out the prescriptions of the Law (see Leviticus 13). The healing occurs on their journey. However, the nine Jews continue their journey; only the Samaritan returns. Significantly he praises God and then throws himself down before God's instrument. In effect, Jesus' question about the nine condemns the religious leadership of Jerusalem. They have failed to make the proper discovery. They have failed to recognize the manifestation of God's power in Jesus. Appropriately, Jesus concludes by remarking that the Samaritan's faith has healed him. It is not simply the belief that Jesus can heal; the nine had that. It is the dimension of faith that recognizes not only the gift but also the giver. Thus the Samaritan has a double gain: health and acceptance of Jesus.

Jesus Presents the Parable of the Persistent Widow (18:1-8)

This parable of the unjust judge may look back to the problem of survival during persecution, a problem discussed in the day of the Son of Man (see 17:22-36). What should be the attitude of the believer when crises come and persecutions abound? Should a person simply sit down and wait for Jesus' return? Verse 1 does not reply that perseverance ultimately fulfils one's prayer. It does reply that constancy will counteract capitulation and that God will never cease to support his followers.

The judge in question has no regard for what either God or people say about him. The woman in question is a widow. Hence, her survival is precarious in a male-dominated society. Her virtue, however, is perseverance. She is so persistent that she gets on the judge's nerves. As a result, he is forced to vindicate her lest her obstinacy completely wear him down.

In verses 7-8 Luke has Jesus apply the parable against the background of persecution and temptation to infidelity. With regard to the first question (v 7a), God who is Father will obviously heed his elect if they continue to cry out. With regard to the second question (v 7b), God will indeed be patient with those tempted to infidelity, although faith may very likely grow thin before Jesus' return.

Jesus Presents the Parable of the Pharisee and the Tax Collector (18:9-14)

Part of the background of this parable is the proper spirit of prayer that should characterize all kingdom seekers. Although Luke mentions the Pharisee, his audience is wider (see 18:7-8). In the parable both the Pharisee and the hated tax collector (hence 'sinner') adopt the same liturgical position (standing) and invoke the same God. They also employ acceptable liturgical prayer forms: a thanksgiving for the Pharisee (see Psalm 17:1-5) and a lament for the tax collector (see Psalm 51).

The Pharisee's prayer soon becomes a catalogue of his own achievements, a litany of his own praises. His prayer stresses, not that he is less than God, but that he is more than others, especially the tax collector. His prayer has degenerated into the accolades of his world; it has not penetrated the reality of God's world. The tax collector's prayer, however, is a humble recital of faults and an inventory of sins ('beat his breast'). His prayer obviously states that he is less than God ('me a sinner'). But there is no purpose in further comparison. By such a prayer the tax collector is in contact with God's (and hence humankind's) real world – a world where honesty undoes sin. Jesus judges that the tax collector went home right with God ('justified') whereas the Pharisee went home only right with himself. In the kingdom only those right with God, not themselves, make it.

Jesus Summons Zaccheus the Tax Collector (19:1-10)

The Zacchaeus story is unique to Luke. He has inserted it between the healing of Bartimaeus (18:35-43) and the parable of the sums of money (19:11-27). It is likely that Luke is attempting to make explicit the implicit element in the Bartimaeus story, namely, forgiveness as the granting of salvation.

Luke emphasizes that Zacchaeus is a chief tax collector. Although tax collectors are admittedly sinners (see 3:12), Jesus seeks out their company (7:34). Moreover, Zacchaeus is a wealthy man – he is, humanly speaking, unable to enter the kingdom (12:16-31). Yet Zacchaeus is small of stature and the little people are apt citizens of the kingdom (9:48; 18:17). By using the word 'today' twice (vv 5, 9), Luke shows the presence of salvation in the figure of Jesus (2:11; 23:43). Indeed, his coming to Zacchaeus' house is part of the Father's plan. Jesus admits that he must indeed stay at his house. His arrival there is an instance of Jesus' mercy and forgiveness ('the Son of Man has come to seek and save what was lost').

This story is also an example of Jesus' overcoming of the objections of the crowd (v 7). Luke points out that, to be saved, one must accept Jesus' offer of table fellowship, make up for any injustices (v 8), and welcome Jesus into one's house.

The Ministry of Jesus in Jerusalem (19:28 – 21:38)

Jesus Explains the Meaning of Resurrection (20:27-38)

In this section of the gospel Jesus concludes his journey by entering Jerusalem, the city of destiny. Here Luke portrays Jesus uttering his lament over the doomed capital (19:41-44). His arrival there is intended to offer peace. However, the rejection of the Prophet will only lead to its destruction. Jesus next proceeds to cleanse the temple (19:45-46). Luke then goes on to state that he taught every day in the temple but that the chief priests, the scribes, and the Jewish leadership are seeking to destroy him. These efforts prove to be unsuccessful. Ironically, while Jesus engages in disputes with his opponents, all the people are hanging on his every word.

After encountering the chief priests, scribes, and elders (20:1-26), Jesus now does battle with the Sadducees. They were the priestly party that emerged during the Maccabean period and opposed the Pharisees by excluding all oral interpretation of the Law. They were the conservatives who denied belief in the resurrection and the existence of angels (see Acts 23:8). In this passage (vv 28-32) the Sadducees use the levirate law of Deuteronomy 25:5-10 to support their case for denying the resurrection. If there is such a thing as resurrection, then to which of the seven brothers does the woman belong in this hypothetical case?

Jesus replies that his opponents have confused the present age with the future age, *i.e.*, marriage is in view of the present, not the future. Moreover, resurrection is only for those judged worthy (v 36). Moses was concerned with posterity, but in the resurrection there is no question of death. Aware of their denial of the existence of angels, Jesus observes that those who share in the resurrection become like angels (see Mark 12:25) and are sons of God (a title used for angels in Genesis 6:2 and Job 1:6). If the resurrected are called sons of God, then why deny the existence of angels who are also called sons of God?

In citing the passage about the burning bush (Exodus 3:6), Jesus shows that God is the God of the living since the patriarchs were long dead at the time the account of the Exodus was composed. Here Luke adds (see Mark 12:27) that all are alive for God.

It is possible that Luke is drawing on non-canonical Fourth Maccabees. In 16:25 the author of that work says that the Maccabean mother and her seven sons, although dead, live unto God with Abraham, Isaac, and Jacob.

Jesus Describes the End-time and the Proper Conduct of His Followers (21:5-19)

Luke divides this section of Jesus' end-time message into two parts: (1) false messiahs and great disasters (vv 6, 8-11); and (2) persecution and testimony of the disciples (vv 12-19). For Luke it is very important to separate the destruction of Jerusalem from the signs of the end time. Thus he removes all eschatological references from this discourse. (See 17:20-37, where he presents the *parousia* or second coming discourse, separating what Matthew 24 and Mark 13 combine, namely, the fall of Jerusalem and the parousia.)

'I am he' (v 8) is a divine title in the Old Testament (see Exodus 3:14; Isaiah 43:10-11). Some will claim to be the Messiah. Others will claim that spectacular events indicate that history is approaching its consummation. Luke's reply to such assertions is that there is no obvious timetable.

Prior to the spectacular events (contrast Mark 13:8-10), the Church will suffer persecution. However, this will be the opportunity to bear witness. In such crises the proper word and wisdom will be forthcoming (see 12:11-12), for the Spirit will be at work (Acts 6:10). In the face of opposition from family, friends, and indeed from almost any quarter, the faithful will find security. Patient endurance will win out. Even if some may have to surrender their lives, they will not thereby lose their real selves.

Jesus Describes the Coming of the Son of Man and Calls for Vigilance (21:25-28, 34-36)

In this passage Luke warns his audience that there is no precise, definite date for Jesus' second coming (*parousia*). Even though Jerusalem was destroyed in 70 A.D. and with it the temple, still that does not herald the second coming. Even contemporary persecutions are not certain signs that the end has come. Christians, therefore, have to adjust to a longer period of waiting.

Verses 25-26 are in apocalyptic language (see Mark 13:24-25) that has much in common with Isaiah 13:9-10. It develops the prophetic notion of the Day of the Lord (see Amos 5:18-20). It is a day of vengeance on the oppressors of God's people and a day of redemption for the oppressed. At that time the Gentile armies will be overthrown, but the loyal subjects of God will be vindicated.

Whereas Mark 13:26 speaks of the Son of Man coming on the clouds, Luke speaks only of a cloud (v 27). This is probably to be connected with the cloud at the transfiguration (9:34) and at the ascension (Acts 1:9-11). Hence there is a link between past and future events. When that future event takes place, his audience will know that their 'redemption' has arrived. 'Redemption' is rooted in the Old Testament experience of liberation. Jesus will come to liberate the faithful.

In the final section of this passage Luke exhorts his audience to be vigilant. The delay of the *parousia* is no reason for giving up vigilance. Constant prayer is Luke's recommendation for coping with all the dangers to which his audience is subject. Through constant prayer and vigilance they will have no reason to fear appearing before the Son of Man in his second coming.

The Passion Narrative (22:1 – 23:56a)

Luke Narrates the Events surrounding Jesus's Passion and Death (22:1–23:56a)

For Luke, Jesus' passion holds transforming power. The memory of the first Passover and its ritual provide the background for Jesus' interpretation of his death, namely, one that will transform others. For example, the healing of the ear of the servant of the high priest (22:51), Jesus' glance at Peter after his denial (22:61), the forgiveness extended to his executioners (23:34), and the promise of paradise to the repentant criminal (23:43) illustrate the transformative power of Jesus' suffering and death. They are liberating events reminiscent of the original Passover experience.

At the time of the passion Satan returns (22:3). Hence Jesus' conflict is with the powers of darkness (22:53), not simply with the Jewish leadership. Satan's effort is to thwart God's plan, yet Jesus counters by proceeding according to his appointed course (22:22). At the Last Supper Jesus returns to the Father's plan. The text about the prophet/servant (Isaiah 53:12) has to be fulfilled (22:37). In the garden Jesus prays only once, but it provides the community with the model of prayer in the face of martyrdom (22:41-44).

Pilate acknowledges Jesus' innocence three times (23:4,14-15 and, even when handing him over to be crucified, does not pronounce him guilty (23:24-25). Both a pagan (Pilate) and a Jew (Herod) agree on his innocence. Luke alone distinguishes the two criminals (23:40-41) and has the repentant criminal acknowledge Jesus' innocence. Finally, the centurion offers this testimony: 'This man was innocent beyond doubt' (23:47).

Luke insists on Jesus' prophetic role here. He is the Prophet who fearlessly proclaims God's justice and gives faithful witness even in the face of rejection and death. He fulfills his prophetic destiny that he expressed earlier when he said: 'it is impossible that a prophet should die outside of Jerusalem' (13:33). Even when accused by the Sanhedrin, Jesus speaks boldly without flinching (22:67-70). Pursuing his prophetic role, he addresses a woe oracle to the women on the way of the cross (23:27-31). He also suffers the taunts of his torturers who challenge him to prophesy (22:63-64).

Jesus Acts Regally by Pardoning the Good Thief (23:35-43)

This passage deals with the theme of kingship. Crucifixion between two criminals (v 33) conjures up the image of a king with two of his cabinet officers (see Mark 10:37). The mockery of the rulers ('the Christ of God') suggests the temptation scene in 4:1-13 where Jesus is prevailed upon to do it the easy way. The soldiers also heap ridicule on the king by their gift of wine. The inscription ('the King of the Jews') is another element in the mockery. The soldiers, like Satan in the desert, are provoking a demonstration of royalty (4:5-7) from the royal figure enthroned on the cross. The unrepentant criminal also pursues the false implications of messiahship, namely, the deliverance of all three criminals.

The repentant criminal is Luke's means of underlining the innocence of Jesus. Here Luke emphasizes the heinousness of killing an innocent king. The name 'Jesus' (v 42) refers to his royal dignity (see 1:31) that this monarch will assume only upon his death. 'Today' (v 43) is a key theological statement in Luke. It looks back to the earlier 'todays,' *e.g.*, the Messiah born in Bethlehem (2:11) and the scripture fulfilled in Nazareth (4:21). As king, Jesus chooses to associate with outcasts like Zacchaeus – there 'today' appears twice (19:5,9). In the elite company of the king the repentant criminal enters the royal estate (Paradise).

Resurrection Narratives
(23:56b – 24:53)

Two Men Announce the Resurrction of Jesus to the Women (24:1-12)

A typical feature of the Christian resurrection accounts is the commanding word of Jesus. Perhaps more significantly, these accounts are more than random stories. Rather, they are the building blocks of the Christian community, *i.e.*, they are constitutive of that community. In his gospel Luke provides an assortment of stories: (1) an empty tomb story (24:1-12); a 'recognition' story in the account of the Emmaus travellers (24:13-35); (3) an appearance to all the disciples gathered together (24:36-49); and (4) an ascension story (24:50-53). (In Acts 1:9-11 Luke provides a second ascension account.)

It is important to note that Luke confines his resurrection appearances to Jerusalem or its vicinity. Hence there are no appearances or promises of appearances in Galilee. In Jesus' appearances Luke emphasizes the theme of the fulfilment of prophecy. In addition, these gospel appearances anticipate the Acts of the Apostles and the ministry of the apostles there.

Luke's empty tomb story is a study in contrasts. The women are authoritative witnesses, but they do not arrive at faith (vv 1-3). The two men scold the women for failing to understand the message of Jesus that spoke of his resurrection (vv 4-7). The women report their findings to the Eleven and others, but are met with ridicule (vv 8-11). Finally the authority of the group, Peter, is overawed by his own visit to the tomb but still unable to grasp the meaning of the event. Perplexity, disbelief, bewilderment - these characterize the figures in the drama.

The women play a significant role in Luke and a much more positive one when compared with Luke's source Mark. From 8:1-3 on they have been members of Jesus' entourage in Galilee. Luke notes that the women were present at the crucifixion (23:49) and that they observed not only where (Mark 15:47) but also how the body of Jesus was laid in the tomb (23:55). Their great failing is not to find the body of Jesus. Their experience engenders perplexity, not a faith understanding of the facts.

The two men are clearly linked with the transfiguration (9:30). On that occasion Moses and Elijah discussed the destiny of the Messiah. 'What he said' (v 6) and 'his words' (v 8) refer to Jesus' prophecy about his passion, death, and resurrection. However, the meaning eluded the disciples (18:34). The repetition of the passion statement here (v 7) suggests that the message of Easter is to reveal the mystery of the Messiah's program. It is part of God's plan that Jesus must suffer. Only the presence of the risen

Lord will evoke faith (24:26,44).

The women return to the authoritative gathering of the Eleven and others. The credentials and number of the observers are excellent. But the women's report of the phenomena does not awaken faith, only ridicule and disbelief. To round out the story, Peter goes to the tomb. But once again, incomprehension and amazement are the result. Only the commanding presence of the Lord will make Peter a believer (24:34).

Jesus Encounters the Emmaus Travellers (24:13-35)

This passage may be divided as follows: (1) introduction, involving the journey and encounter with Jesus (vv 13-15); (2) body (vv 16-31), moving from non-recognition (v 16) to recognition (v 31); and (3) conclusion, containing the reaction of the two disciples and their return to Jerusalem (vv 32-35).

In the body of the text there are two components: (a) dialogue narrative (vv 17-27); and (2) meal narrative (vv 28-30). (This may reflect the structure of the early Christian assemblies, namely, discourse followed by a meal.) The dialogue (vv 19-20) first notes the acceptance of Jesus but observes that such acceptance ended in tragedy. Next (v 21), the two disciples give expression to their personal hopes. And finally (vv 22-23) they mention the report of the women at the tomb. Jesus then responds (vv 25-27) by expounding the Scriptures, especially the nexus between tragedy and glory. In the meal narrative the guest performs the tasks of the host. The language of blessing, breaking, and distributing has Eucharistic overtones. For Luke's audience Jesus is both guest and host at the Christian meal. Luke suggests that those who share with others can rediscover the risen Lord and thus regain lost hope.

In the conclusion the disciples acknowledge the impact of Jesus' interpretation. In turn, they are moved to communicate it to others. They repeat the recognition theme, i.e., the breaking of the bread reveals the person of the risen Lord.

The Risen Jesus Appears to the Apostolic Circle (24:35-48)

This passage is part of Luke's account of the appearance of Jesus to the apostolic circle (24:36-53). It may be divided as follows: (1) appearance (vv 36-43); and (2) instruction (vv 44-49). What emerges from the account is Luke's insistence on the necessity of the revealing word.

In the appearance scene Jesus is the prototype of the Christian missionary. The peace greeting and the acceptance of food from the community are, for Luke, part of the itinerant missionary's life (see 10:5-7).

The household meal is particularly significant since it is related to Jesus' meal scenes where forgiveness of sins is prominent (5:32; 7:39,48; 19:10). While 'it is I myself' (v 39) announces the identity of the risen Christ with the earthly Jesus, Luke nonetheless postpones the disciples' recognition of Jesus until the ascension scene (v 53). For Luke, presence must be coupled with the revealing word.

In the instruction scene Luke has Jesus once again unravel the meaning of the Scriptures (v 45). Luke's emphasis on divine necessity covers: (1) passion and glory (v 46); and (2) universal preaching (v 47). The missionary preaches 'in his name' and is a witness. For the evangelist these terms envision more than being a guarantor of the events. They connote re-enacting Jesus' journey (9:51) and sharing in his prophetic status. Facts are not enough. The meaning of the facts must be exemplified in the missionary.

Jesus Ascends into Heaven (24:46-53)

As noted above, this passage is part of Luke's account of the appearance of Jesus to the apostolic circle (24:36-53). It may be divided as follows: (1) appearance (vv 36-43); (2) instruction (vv 44-49); and (3) ascension (vv 50-53).

In the instruction scene Luke has Jesus once again unravel the meaning of the Scriptures (vv 45-46). Luke's emphasis on divine necessity covers: (1) passion and glory (v 46); and (2) universal preaching (v 47). The missionary preaches 'in his name' and is a witness. For Luke these terms envision more than being a guarantor of the events. They connote reenacting Jesus' journey (9:51) and sharing in his prophetic status. Facts are not enough. The meaning of the facts must be exemplified in the missionary. Verse 49 mentions the promise of the Father and 'power from on high.' According to Acts 1:8 this promise and power is the Holy Spirit. The command to remain in the city conjures up the future suffering of the missionary since Jerusalem traditionally persecutes God's emissaries.

Luke has modelled the ascension account on Sirach 50:20-23 that describes the glory of the high priest Simon II. In the temple Simon would officiate, coming down and raising his hands to give the blessing. The people would then lie prostrate to receive the blessing. Sirach would then exhort the people to bless God and would pray that they have joy of heart. Jesus' departure in this gospel passage is thus after the manner of the high priest who blesses. At Jesus' ascension the disciples are prostrate but then return to Jerusalem filled with joy. As in Sirach, they are in the temple, praising God.

Significantly, the scene in Sirach 50 is the finale of the 'Praise of the Fathers' (Sir 44–50). The great miracles performed by the Fathers were the fruits of a prophetic heritage that went back to Moses. Jesus, therefore, is the end of Israel's history interpreted as prophecy.

Concluding Reflections on the Jesus of Luke

For Luke Jesus is the Prophet, *i.e.*, God's unique spokesperson to Israel and ultimately to the Gentiles. Although Luke presents Jesus as a prophetic figure of that kind at his baptism (3:22), it is especially at the inaugural address in the Nazareth synagogue that Jesus publicly assumes this office. On that occasion the passages from Isaiah are fulfilled in Jesus (4:21). This scene, however, also has negative overtones in that Jesus experiences prophetic rejection at the hands of his townspeople (4:28-30). He expresses this outcome publicly when he declares that a prophet must indeed die in Jerusalem (13:33). Divine necessity (glory by way of tragedy) overshadows his entire prophetic career. His miracles also announce his prophetic role when, for example, his raising of the widow's son in Nain moves the funeral participants to exclaim that a great prophet has indeed arisen in their midst (7:16).

Luke has greatly expanded Mark's account of Jesus' journey to Jerusalem. Like the prophet Ezekiel, he sets his face toward Jerusalem, the city of destiny (9:51). Absolutely nothing at all will distract him from achieving this goal. As he announces in 13:33, 'I must continue on my way today, tomorrow, and the following day ... ' Luke takes pains to associate Jesus' disciples with this journey. However, joining Jesus on this trek is no easy matter. Nothing less than wholehearted commitment will do (9:57-62). There is no turning back!

Luke insists upon making Jesus the model of prayer. He also seems to go out of his way to underline this central role of prayer in the life of the disciple. At his baptism (3:21), in his selection of the Twelve (6:12), at Peter's confession (9:18), at his transfiguration (9:28), prior to giving the Our Father (11:1), during his agony in the garden (22:41), and on the cross (23:46) Jesus is communing with his Father in prayer. For his Gentile-Christian audience Luke makes prayer, especially prayer of petition, an absolutely essential element for the disciple of Jesus. It is hardly by accident that Luke begins (1:10) and ends (24:53) his gospel with prayer in the Jerusalem temple.

The Jesus of Luke speaks more emphatically about the disciple's proper use of material possessions, wealth, and money than the other three evangelists. This emphasis suggests that Luke has experienced problems about this dimension of discipleship in his own community. To counteract such abuses, the Jesus of Luke does not hesitate to make radical demands on his followers. Whereas in Mark 1:20 the first four disciples leave Zebedee in the boat with the hired hands, in Luke they leave everything (5:11). Whereas the rich young man in Mark 10:21 is told to sell what he has and give to the poor, the rich official in Luke is told to sell all that he has and distribute it to the poor (18:27). The Jesus of Luke insists on the proper use of material possessions right from the start of the gospel. In her *Magnificat* Mary sings about how God has filled the hungry with good things but has sent the rich away empty (1:53). In preaching to the crowds, John the Baptist instructs them as well as the tax collectors and soldiers about the proper use of money and material possessions (3:10-14). As Luke's Sermon on the Plain indicates, his Jesus is concerned about the economically and socially poor (6:20,24; contrast Matthew 5:3). The parable of the rich fool (12:16-21) and the parable of the rich man and Lazarus (16:19-26) – both unique to Luke – focus on the issues of wealth and concern for others. Finally, it should be noted that for the Jesus of Luke 'poor' also includes the downtrodden, the rejected, and the persecuted as well as prisoners.

Luke mentions the role of the Spirit more frequently than all the other evangelists. This is especially true of the beginning of his gospel. There are seven occurrences in the infancy narrative and six in the next two chapters. The Spirit expresses God's presence to his people in active, creative, and prophetic ways. Luke portrays his Jesus as the bearer of God's Spirit to humanity. It is hardly surprising, therefore, that Jesus cites this passage from Isaiah 61:1 in his inaugural address: 'The Spirit of the Lord is upon me' (4:18). The Spirit thus empowers Jesus the Prophet to carry out his mission.

The Jesus of John

The Setting of the Gospel of John

Writing in the late first Christian century, probably between 90 and 100, the author of the Fourth Gospel tells an old story in a new way. The place of composition is often thought to be Ephesus (modern western Turkey). Traditionally, the author was believed to be John, the son of Zebedee and brother of James – hence a member of the Twelve and an eyewitness to the events narrated in the gospel. In current scholarship the author is thought to be a gifted theologian who was a member of the Johannine community and thus had access to the special traditions of that community.

In this gospel the Beloved Disciple plays a key role. While probably a relatively minor figure during Jesus' ministry, this person became singularly important in the history of the Johannine community and functions as the model disciple in this gospel, even able to serve as a contrast to Peter as closer to Jesus in love. Although not the author of this gospel (despite 21:20,24), the Beloved Disciple functions as the bearer and guarantor of the many rich traditions in this composition. (In the following commentary 'John' represents the author of this gospel, although his identity cannot be further determined.)

The tradition behind John is solidly rooted in Palestine. For example, the author mentions sites not found in the other gospels, some of which have been verified (Solomon's portico in the temple [10:23], the pool of Bethesda [5:2], and the pool of Siloam [9:7]). The author is also familiar with Jewish feasts (6:4; 10:22) and customs (2:6; 19:36).

However, the presentation of these traditions reflects a period beyond Jesus' ministry. By this time Christians have been expelled from the synagogue (9:22). 'The Jews' are by this time a group separate from Christians and enormously disliked. Unlike in the Synoptics (Matthew, Mark, and Luke – so-called because they share a common viewpoint), the Jesus of John does not hesitate to speak of his divine status (8:58; 10:30) and pre-existence (17:4). The first conclusion of this gospel even states that the purpose of this writing is to evoke the belief that 'Jesus is the Christ, the Son of God' (20:31). Such development suggests a considerably long period of reflection on the traditions associated with the Beloved Disciple and expansion over many years owing to the experiences of the Johannine community.

In his preaching in this gospel Jesus focuses on himself and his mission as Revealer and Revelation of God. This Jesus reveals who God is and what God expects of disciples. While the notion of kingdom plays a paramount role in the Synoptics, there is relatively little mention of it in John simply because Jesus himself is the very embodiment of the kingdom. In John, Jesus also prefers to speak of his 'hour,' *i.e.*, a single event that brings together his passion, death, resurrection, and exaltation. While Jesus is the Teacher in Matthew owing to his five great sermons, Jesus functions as Revealer and Revelation by means of long discourses. On several occasions what begins as a dialogue ends up as a monologue (see the Farewell Discourse in chapters 14--17).

This gospel may be outlined as follows. First, there is a prologue that introduces several of the key themes of this composition (1:1-18). Second, there is the Book of Signs (1:19–12:50). 'Sign' is the Johannine term for miracle that emphasizes the significance of the event for believers, not the spectacular feat itself. There are seven such signs in this section but they do not include exorcisms. Third, there is the Book of Glory (13:1–20:31). This section contains Jesus' Farewell Discourses at the Last Supper (13:1–17:26), the passion, death, and resurrection narratives (18:1–20:29), and a first conclusion (20:30-31). Fourth, there is an epilogue (21:1-23) containing Galilean resurrection appearances and a second conclusion (21:24-25).

Prologue
(1:1-18)

The Pre-existent Word Becomes Human and Reveals His Glory (1:1-18)

The prologue of John is a hymn that is probably an independent composition stemming from Johannine circles. Moreover, an editor or editors have inserted material into the hymn for two purposes: (1) to explain the hymn more fully (vv 12b-13,17-18) and (2) to distinguish the roles of Jesus and John the Baptist (vv 6-9,15).

While the title 'Word' has prophetic overtones, it is probably best explained here as personified wisdom. Thus Wisdom is with God from the beginning (see Proverbs 8:22-23; Wisdom 6:22). Wisdom reflects the glory and the everlasting light of God (see Wisdom 7:25-26). Wisdom also provokes decisions (see Proverbs 8:17), witht the result that some reject her (Proverbs 1:24-25). As the Word, Jesus is God's Wisdom who is with God from the beginning, reflects God's glory, and challenges people to make a decision for or against God.

The hymn opens with pre-creation and the relationship of the Word to God. By creation (Genesis 1:1: 'in the beginning') that is an act of revelation, the Word has a claim on all. What emerges from God's creative Word is the gift of eternal life. In keeping with Genesis 1:3, the light shines on in darkness, even though humans have sinned. Verses 10-12a refer to the Word incarnate in the ministry of Jesus. Verse 11 sums up the Book of Signs, namely, the rejection of the Word. Verse 12a sums up the Book of Glory, namely, the acceptance of the Word. In verse 14 the Word is bound up with human history and human destiny. 'Made his dwelling' refers to God's tabernacling at Sinai, where God's glory fills the tent (see Exodus 40:34). However, it may also suggest Lady Wisdom's tabernacling in the midst of Israel (see Sirach 24:8). 'Full of grace and truth ' (v 14) implies that believers share in this new wealth of God's steadfast love and fidelity. 'Grace in place of grace' (v 16) seems to suggest that a new covenant relationship is in place.

Verses 6-9, 15 distinguish the roles of Jesus and John the Baptist. The Baptist is a witness to the light; he is not the light. In verse 15 the editor has borrowed from 1:30 to underline the pre-existence of the Word. Verses 12b-13, 17-18 are explanatory additions. Verse 17 is a clearer expression of the 'grace and truth' that comes with the Word. Verse 18 shows that Moses, unlike the Word, never saw God.

The Book of Signs
(1:19 – 12:50)

John the Baptist Answers Questions
Posed by Different Groups (1:6-8, 19-28)

Verses 6-8 are an editor's insertion into the prologue to explain the role of John the Baptist. John is a witness to the light; hence he has a subordinate role in relationship to Jesus.

There are two sets of interrogations in verses 19-27. In the first set (vv 19-23) the Baptist responds negatively, rejecting identification with the traditional figures of the end time, namely, the Christ (Messiah), Elijah, and the Prophet (the prophet like Moses in Deuteronomy 18:15-18). He then responds positively by identifying himself as the herald of Isaiah 40:3. He thereby identifies only in terms of the one who is to come.

In the second set (vv 24-27) the priests and the Levites seek John's reason for baptizing. The Baptist replies that he baptizes only with water (in 1:33 John states that Jesus will baptize with the Holy Spirit). John also refers to the hidden Messiah (v 26: 'whom you do not recognize'), *i.e.*, the

Messiah's presence would be unknown until he suddenly appears among his people. (In 1:33 John admits that only God's help enabled him to recognize Jesus.) The Baptist thus defends his practice of baptizing as a means of preparing for the one to come.

John the Baptist Testifies to the Lamb of God (1:29-34)

In this passage the author of John has skillfully combined the sayings of the Baptist with his theological viewpoint. As it now stands, John identifies Jesus as the Lamb of God (v 29), the Pre-existent One (v 30), and the giver of the Spirit (vv 32-34). While the Baptist probably understands the lamb to mean the apocalyptic lamb who will wipe out God's enemies (see Revelation 7:17; 17:14), the author probably takes it to mean the Suffering Servant (compare Isaiah 53:7 with Isaiah 42:1, *i.e.*, 'chosen one' and 'spirit'). He may also understand the Passover lamb as well (19:13,36). For the Baptist, the Pre-existent One was perhaps Elijah (see Malachi 3:1; Matthew 3:12). However, for the author of John the Pre-existent One is the Word of the prologue.

The author of John does not mention the actual baptism of Jesus. Like Mark (but unlike Matthew and Luke), he speaks of 'Spirit,' not 'Holy Spirit.' Once again the Baptist appears to be referring to the fiery eschatological preacher of judgment (see Matthew 3:11-12; Luke 3:16-17). The author of John, however, understands 'Spirit' as the 'Holy Spirit' that Jesus will communicate to all believers at the moment of his exaltation.

According to 5:31-40 there are different channels through which God's testimony to Jesus is conveyed. The Baptist figures prominently as the first such channel.

Jesus Gathers His First Disciples (1:35-42)

This passage is the Johannine account of the call of the first disciples. Here the Baptist's disciples become Jesus' disciples (see 3:30). The use of the verb 'to follow' (vv 37,38,40) emphasizes the dedication of the disciple. Jesus takes the initiative by inquiring into the object of their quest. That object is God and the verb 'to stay' suggests a permanent, not a temporary commitment. In John the verbs 'to come' and 'to see' are often linked to the process of coming to faith (see 5:50; 6:40,47). Here John uses the motif of Lady Wisdom. For example, in Wisdom 6:16 Wisdom makes her rounds, seeking those who are worthy of her (see Proverbs 1:20-28). To find Wisdom is to find life (Proverbs 8:35).

The day with Jesus leads the two disciples to a deeper insight as to who Jesus really is. Thus Andrew, when speaking with his brother, refers to Jesus as the Messiah. Unlike Matthew 16:16-18 that relates the change of Peter's name (and hence his destiny) much later in the ministry, the author of John places the scene right in the very beginning. John merely states that the basis for the change is Jesus' looking at Peter (v 42). Peter thus begins the process of an ever deeper realization of who and what Jesus actually is.

Jesus Changes Water into Wine at Cana (2:1-12)

This account of the wedding feast of Cana is part of the Book of Signs. For John, a sign is a manifestation of divine glory, and one must look beyond the spectacular event to discover its meaning and value. Although it is very difficult to reconstruct this scene historically, what does emerge is the revelation of the person of Jesus and the belief of his disciples.

The wine – some 120 gallons – has a christological purpose, *i.e.*, it tells the reader something about the person and mission of Jesus. Here Jesus fulfills or brings to completion the meaning of Jewish feasts and practices – in this instance the prescriptions of Jewish purification – with an abundance of wine. In this process of fulfillment or completion Jesus becomes the only way to the Father. The wedding feast symbolizes messianic days. In Isaiah 62:4-5 the author speaks of the coming marriage between the Lord and Jerusalem (see also Isaiah 54:4-8). Amos 9:13-14 refers to the abundance of wine that will characterize 'the coming days' (see also Hosea 14:8). John may also be alluding to Jesus' role as Wisdom in Proverbs 9:5 where Lady Wisdom invites her disciples to drink of her wine.

Mary (designated here as the mother of Jesus) also plays a symbolic role here. She is the New Eve, the symbol of the Church. The next time Mary appears in John is in the scene on Calvary (19:20) where Jesus again addresses her with the polite title of 'woman'. There, as in Revelation 12, Mary is given offspring to protect. It is only at the 'hour' of the passion-death-resurrection-exaltation that she will have a role to play. Up to that moment she has no part in the ministry of Jesus. Here at Cana, Mary has a part in completing the call of the disciples by provoking the incident that leads to their expression of faith. This use of Mary as a collective personality suggests that tradition recognized in the person of Mary the basis for such symbolism.

Jesus Cleanses the Temple (2:13-25)

Unlike John, the Synoptics (Matthew 21:10-17; Mark 11:15-19; Luke 19:45-46) place the cleansing of the temple shortly before Jesus' death. Some suggest that Jesus gave a warning about the temple on an earlier visit to Jerusalem and that the cleansing itself occurred according to the Synoptic chronology. In any event both John and the Synoptics have independent but parallel traditions.

Here Jesus appears like the prophet Jeremiah who decried the abuses connected with the temple (see Jeremiah 7:1-15; 26:1-19). John also seems to have Zechariah 14:21 in mind with its reference to the second temple: 'No longer will there be merchants [see 'marketplace' in 2:16] in the house of the Lord of hosts on that day.' If those responsible do destroy the temple by defiling it, then Jesus will erect a new temple in a short time ('three days').

The Johannine school adapted and reinterpreted the original event. In verse 17 this school makes use of Psalm 69:10 but changes it to the future: 'Zeal for your house will consume me.' The new interpretation is that Jesus' zeal for the temple will ultimately lead to his death. In verses 21-22 the school understands this new temple to be nothing less than Jesus' resurrection body. The new temple, therefore, will the body of the exalted Jesus.

In verses 24-25 John shows that the belief of the many (v 23) is inadequate. They simply see a miracle worker and nothing more. As God's emissary, Jesus knows the inadequacy of the human condition and the transitory quality of human enthusiasm.

In His Dialogue with Nicodemus Jesus Explains Begetting through the Spirit (3:14-21)

This passage is part of Jesus' dialogue with Nicodemus. Jesus has already pointed out that entering God's kingdom hinges on the outpouring of the Spirit, something that humans cannot achieve on their own (3:5-8). Jesus now explains that the Son must ascend to the Father (3:11-15) and that faith is necessary to benefit from the gift of the Spirit (3:16-21).

Verses 14-15 refer directly to Nicodemus' question. This begetting through the Spirit depends on Jesus' death-resurrection-exaltation. The comparison with Moses' bronze serpent (Numbers 21:9) shows that 'to be lifted up' refers to the crucifixion (see 12:33). But for John this is but the beginning of Jesus' return to the Father that is fulfilled in his exaltation (see 8:28; 12:32). 'Being lifted up' ultimately brings life to all believers (7:37-39).

Verse 16 emphasizes the role of the Father. Like Abraham, he gives his only son, whom he loves, for the benefit of all nations of the earth (Genesis 22:2,12,18). Verse 16 parallels verse 17. In verse 16 the Father's giving of the Son brings eternal life to the believer. In verse 17 the Father's sending of the Son brings salvation for the world. The presence of Jesus, therefore, is calculated to force a decision. Whoever does not accept Jesus in faith is already condemned (v 18). In verses 19-21 John employs the imagery of light and darkness. Humans must make a choice between light and darkness. Their way of life influences the choice: evildoers opt for darkness while those acting in truth opt for light. Jesus is the one who provokes this choice. Those hardened in radical evil (v 20: 'everyone who does wicked things') reject the light. Those accustomed to doing good (v 21: 'whoever lives the truth') bathe in the light.

Jesus Speaks with the Samaritan Woman Who then Impacts the Faith of Her Townspeople (4:4-42)

John's account of the Samaritan woman probably has a historical basis that the author reworked to describe the process of coming to faith in Jesus. The account consists of two scenes and a conclusion.

The first scene (vv 4-26), the dialogue with the woman, contains two parts: (1) the discussion about living water (vv 6-15); and (2) the true worship of the Father (vv 16-26). The woman moves from a crass material understanding of water to a more spiritual one. Proverbs 13:14 and Sirach 24:21, 23-29 suggest that living water is Jesus' revelation or teaching. Ezekiel 36:25-27 suggests and John 6:63; 7:37-39 add that living water is the Spirit communicated by Jesus. The discussion of true worship of the Father results in a worship 'in Spirit and truth' (v 23). The Spirit elevates the believer above the earthly level to worship God properly. For John, the Spirit is the Spirit of Jesus and the Spirit of truth (see 14:17; 15:26).

The second scene (vv 27-38) is the dialogue with the disciples. In the discussion about food the disciples operate on a material level, whereas Jesus speaks on the level of mission (vv 31-34). Jesus then explains the two proverbs by referring to the joy of reaping the harvest, indeed a harvest that they did not see (vv 35-38 – a possible background is the conversion of the Samaritans in Acts 8).

The conclusion (vv 39-42) is the conversion of the townspeople. They accept the word of the woman (hence she is a missionary), then the word of Jesus, and finally they confess Jesus to be the saviour of the world. These foreigners, therefore, are a contrast to the Jews and their limited acceptance of Jesus in 2:23-25. These foreigners have found the saviour of the world.

Jesus Multiplies the Loaves and Fish (6:1-15)

While both the Synoptics and John reflect the Eucharistic symbolism in the account of the multiplication of the loaves and fish ('take, bless/thank, break, give/distribute' – 'break' is missing in John), it is John who exploits this scene for a special 'sign' potential. In John, where signs are perceived only as spectacular events, they do not lead to faith. To lead to faith, the sign must provoke God's presence as revealed in Jesus.

The scene has obvious connections to Moses. Just as Moses goes up the mountain (Sinai), so too Jesus goes up the mountain. Philip's statement (v 7) re-echoes Moses' question in Numbers 11:22: 'Can enough sheep and cattle be slaughtered for them?' Similarly 'the Prophet coming into the world' (v 14) was thought to be a new Moses who would found a new Israel. The sign performed by Jesus makes the audience conclude that Jesus is such a figure. At this point John adds a historical note wanting in the Synoptics, *i.e.*, the people attempt to make Jesus their king because of the sign (v 15). For John, therefore, the sign does not lead the people to recognize the true nature of Jesus. It is 'just' a miracle.

Jesus Identifies Himself as the Bread of Life (6:24-35)

After the sign of the multiplication of the loaves and fish the people search for Jesus and ultimately find him. Jesus does not answer their question about when he got there since they have not perceived the true meaning of the sign. He suggests that the people work for the imperishable food that will lead to eternal life. This involves accepting Jesus in faith.

However, the people think that they are merely to believe in some new sign that Jesus will perform – like the manna in the desert. Jesus counters that it was not Moses but his Father who provided the manna. Moreover, the real heavenly bread that the Father will give is Jesus himself. Alluding to the Israelites in the desert, Jesus explains that anyone who comes to him (and hence believes) will never again hunger or thirst. Jesus reveals himself to the people ('I am the bread of life') as God revealed himself to Moses: 'I am the God of your father' (Exodus 3:6; see also 3:14).

John employs the 'I am' formula in two ways, the first of which is the absolute use. For example, 'When you lift up the Son of Man, you will realize that I AM ... ' (8:28; see also 8:58). This absolute use derives from the Old Testament: see the texts given above from Exodus. In the prophetic literature Second Isaiah also uses this formula: 'I am the Lord, and there is no other' (Isaiah 45:18). Such texts emphasize the unicity of God. In applying this absolute formula to statements by Jesus, John attests to his divine status.

The second way in which John uses the 'I am' formula is the addition of a predicate nominative, *e.g.*, 'I am the bread of life' (6:35) and 'I am the light of the world' (8:12). In this usage John does not exclusively emphasize the 'I' but rather the predicate (bread of life, light of the world). These predicates articulate some dimension of Jesus' relationship to humanity or some aspect of the Father's sending of the Son into the world. Such usage supports the contention that in this gospel Jesus is the Revealer and the Revelation of God.

Jesus Identifies Himself as the Living Bread (6:41-51)

In this passage John has Jesus employ one of life's staples, bread, to symbolize his person and his work. In turn, the symbol is calculated to reveal the Father and his plan. Jesus quotes Isaiah 54:13: 'They shall all be taught by God.' Jesus fulfills this by presenting himself as the one who provides what is contained in the religious symbol of bread. Since bread maintains life, Jesus will maintain life in all who come to him in faith. For their part, the people must look beyond mere human credentials – Jesus' family origins – and perceive him as the manifestation of the Father. At the end of his gospel John connects this bread with Jesus' redemptive death: the bread is his flesh for the life of the world. John thus identifies Jesus' revelation of the Father in terms of his self-giving. To accept Jesus as the living bread is to accept him as the self-giving expression of the Father's love in his death-glorification.

Jesus Explains the Sacramental Dimension of the Symbol of Bread (6:51-58)

In this passage John passes from the use of bread symbolizing Jesus' identity to its sacramental use. It is now a question of eating the flesh and drinking the blood of Jesus. Jesus has not only become flesh, *i.e.*, human (1:14). He also gives his flesh and blood as food and drink for believers. 'Flesh' implies the whole person as mortal and natural. 'Blood' means the entire person as living. John also links Jesus' flesh and blood to the final resurrection: 'Whoever eats my flesh and drinks my blood has eternal life, and I will raise him on the last day' (v 54). Compared to Jesus as the living bread (v 51), the manna in the desert provides only a very weak analogy

John Narrates the Different Reactions to Jesus' Discourse (6:60-69)

In this passage there are different reactions to Jesus' words: murmuring, unwillingness to believe, complete loyalty. On one level some disciples cannot accept that Jesus is the living bread come down from heaven. Obviously they would find it more difficult to accept Jesus' return to the Father. On another level some disciples object to Jesus' statement that the bread he gives is his flesh, *i.e.*, the Eucharist. In any event, disciples need grace to believe on either level.

On the other hand, the Twelve serve as a contrast. They vow their loyalty to Jesus through Simon Peter, their spokesperson. Only Jesus has the words of eternal life. They have arrived at faith: 'We have come to believe and are convinced that you are the Holy One of God' (v 69).

Jesus Announces His Gift of the Spirit at His Glorification (7:37-39)

The Feast of Tabernacles recalled the desert wanderings of the Israelites when they lived in tents (tabernacles) and when God provided not only manna but also water from the rock (see Psalm 78:15-16). The feast also had a special relationship to the temple. Ezekiel 47:1-11 and Zechariah 14:8 spoke of a river of water that would flow out from the Jerusalem temple. On the seventh day of the festival the priest would pour the water taken from the fountain of Gihon into the ground of the temple. Against the agricultural background of the feast it was the occasion to pray for abundant rains.

In this passage Jesus solemnly proclaims that living waters will flow out from his body and be available to all believers. The symbolism of the water appears to be twofold. First, it is the revelation that Jesus will offer to all believers. This is probably linked to Lady Wisdom who will offer her message, her table, to all who will heed her (Proverbs 1:20; 8:2-3; 9:3). Second, according to verse 39 water is the Spirit that the risen Jesus will give. Although the Spirit is active in the life and person of Jesus, it is not communicated to believers until the resurrection of Jesus (that John combines with the ascension and Pentecost). It is only at Easter that Jesus will breathe on the disciples and say: 'Receive the Holy Spirit' (20:22). Hence only the glorification of Jesus can release the Spirit upon the community.

Jesus Forgives the Adulterous Woman (8:1-11)

This story of the adulterous woman was never part of the Gospel of John. Eventually, however, it found its way into the Fourth Gospel. (It is regarded as canonical by the Church.) One reason for the delay may be that Jesus' rather easy way of forgiving conflicted with the stringent penitential practices of the early Christian community. In any event, it is a priceless story demonstrating both Jesus' forgiveness and wisdom.

It is likely, but far from certain, that the situation placed Jesus in a dilemma. On the one hand, the scribes and the Pharisees found the woman guilty and sentenced her to death. On the other hand, the Romans had reserved the use of the death penalty to themselves (see 18:31). If Jesus approves the Jewish sentence, he flies in the face of Roman law. If he disapproves the sentence, he flies in the face of Jewish law. In the account, however, Jesus refuses to answer the question (v 5) simply because it is wrong. The writing on the ground may have been Jesus' doodling to distract the audience. In any event, without condoning adultery, Jesus shows that the proper question is: What is the extent of mercy? To be sure, the accusers had no interest in the purpose of the law: they were there only to test Jesus. The outcome is the disappearance of the accusers and a new orientation: 'Go, and from now on do not sin any more' (v 11).

Jesus Heals the Man Born Blind and Identifies Himself as the Light of the World (9:1-41)

This passage may be outlined as follows: (1) setting (vv 1-5); (2) sign (vv 6-7); (3) various interrogations (vv 8-34); and (4) attainment of spiritual sight, *i.e.*, faith (vv 35-41). In the case of the man born blind, it is the triumph of light over darkness – Jesus thus clearly establishes that he is the light of the world (v 5). While the man advances from darkness to light, the Pharisees / the Jews retrograde from halting acceptance to outright rejection of Jesus. On the one hand, the man first speaks of Jesus as a man (v 11), calls him a prophet (v 17), attests that he comes from God (v 33), and finally acknowledges him as the Son of Man (v 37). On the other hand, the Pharisees / the Jews initially seem to accept the healing (16), but then doubt the blindness from birth (v 18), reject Jesus' heavenly origins (v 29), vilify the man (v 34), and are finally judged to be spiritually blind (vv 39, 41). The man born blind ends up seeing (faith) while the seeing Pharisees/Jews end up blind (lack of faith).

There is an apologetic element in the account. If Jesus does enjoy such special powers, then who is he? Verses 28-33 reflect the polemic towards the end of the first Christian century: the disciples of Moses versus the disciples of Jesus. Verses 22-23, although perhaps written by a later hand, point up the situation, namely, excommunication of disciples of Jesus from the synagogue. The account assures these disciples that Jesus will seek them out, as he sought out the man born blind.

Jesus Identifies Himself as the Sheep-gate (10:1-10)

John 10:1-21 follows Jesus' altercation with the Pharisees over the man born blind (9:1-41) and leads into the dispute with the Jews (10:21-39). This particular passage consists of: (1) two parables (vv 1-3a,3b-5); (2) reaction at the failure to understand (v 6); and (3) explanation of the parables (vv 7-8,9-10).

In the first parable the right way to approach the sheep is by means of the gate opened by the keeper. 'A thief and a robber' (v 1) may refer to the Pharisees in the preceding chapter who do not approach the sheep properly but merely provide for themselves. In the second parable 'leads them out' (v 3b) suggests Ezekiel 34:13 where the Lord in his capacity as shepherd meets the needs of his sheep. According to Numbers 27:16-17 Joshua (rendered 'Jesus' in Greek) guides the community so that they are not like sheep without a shepherd (see Mark 6:34). Sheep will not follow a stranger, not unlike the man born blind who refuses to follow the Pharisees.

In the first explanation only Jesus is the sheep-gate by which the sheep can be approached. 'All who came before me' (v 8) may allude to the leaders, from Maccabean times on, who pastured themselves, not the sheep. In the second explanation (only loosely connected with vv 1-3a), only Jesus is the gate that leads to salvation. However, it is a gate for the sheep, not the shepherds. Jesus brings life to the sheep, the thief brings death. Jesus identifies in terms of the sheep, the thief in terms of himself.

Jesus Identifies Himself as the Good Shepherd (10:11-18)

This passage also reflects an atmosphere of conflict as it follows upon the account of the Pharisees' rejection of the man born blind. Jesus, therefore, contrasts himself with these leaders of Israel. 'Shepherd' bears all the connotations of authority and, therefore, responsibility, implying complete dedication to those in one's charge.

There are two parables about the good or ideal shepherd: (1) verses 11-13; and (2) verses 14-16. In the first parable Jesus is the ideal shepherd because he does not shrink from laying down his life for his sheep. (The image suggests a combination of shepherd and Suffering Servant.) Given the context, it is likely that the hired hands are the Pharisees. In the second parable Jesus is the ideal shepherd because he knows his sheep. As in 1 John 3:1, this knowledge implies a deep personal relationship between shepherd and sheep. According to verse 16, the goal of this knowing is to bring about union among all of Jesus' followers – hence a reference to the Gentile mission.

Verses 17-18 are outside the parable and perhaps link the Gentile mission to the death/resurrection of Jesus. In Johannine theology, since the Father and the Son have the same power (10:28-30), Jesus' rising from the dead is the same as the Father's raising Jesus from the dead (see Acts 4:10). Verse 18 shows that the death/resurrection of Jesus is tied to the Father's will. In dying, Jesus freely opens himself up to taking up his life again.

Jesus Announces His Union with the Father (10:27-30)

This passage is part of John's larger scene dealing with Jesus' replies to his enemies on the feast of Dedication or Hanukkah (10:22-39). In the first exchange we have the question (v 24: 'If you are the Messiah') followed by

Jesus' reply that culminates in a declaration of his union with the Father (vv 25-30). This in turn is followed by an unfavorable reaction on the part of the Jews, namely, the attempt to stone Jesus (v 31).

Jesus responds to the Jews in terms of shepherd/sheep. Kings in the ancient Near East were often called shepherds. The Davidic kings, who were anointed (= Messiah), also bore the title of shepherd (see Ezekiel 34:1-31). Jesus apparently could not buy the excessive political and nationalistic overtones of some popular messianic thinking.

In this passage he replies to his opponents that they remain unconvinced by his works because they are not sheep who hear his voice. On the other hand, those who are his sheep (10:4) recognize him and follow him. Unlike the hireling (10:12), Jesus will not allow wolves to snatch his sheep (see Isaiah 43:13). There is, therefore, a union existing between the Father and Jesus. That union is the bond by which Jesus will bind people to himself. Admittedly, Jesus is a different type of shepherd.

Jesus Identifies Himself as the Resurrection and the Life (11:1-45)

John probably takes a miracle from Jesus' ministry (the raising of a dead man to life) and, unlike the Synoptics, makes this one sign the reason for his condemnation (see 11:45-54). Moreover, just as the healing of the man born blind shows that Jesus is the light, the raising of Lazarus demonstrates that Jesus is the life. The account may be outlined as follows: (1) setting (vv 1-6); (2) questions about the journey (vv 7-16); (3) Martha and Jesus (vv 17-27); (4) Mary and Jesus (vv 28-33); and (5) the raising of Lazarus (34-44). (Verse 45 is the start of the next section.)

Martha's character is in keeping with Luke's description (see Luke 10:38-42). Though she is a person of faith, she does not yet believe that Jesus is life itself (v 25). Indeed she sees him merely as an extraordinary mediator between God and her personal plight. Even when Jesus replies that he is life itself, Martha misunderstands, limiting her vision to the resurrection on the last day (v 24). Jesus' reply is to state categorically that the believer will live on another level, even though such a person has experienced physical death. To live on such a level is to preclude all separation from community with God. For John, belief in Jesus is the gift of eternal life. The raising of Lazarus demonstrates this.

This account points up the interconnection of faith and glory. Verse 4 states that this sign will glorify Jesus (his death is the catalyst for glory). Verse 15 emphasizes that the miracle envisions the disciple's faith. Verse 40 affirms that faith will lead to the display of God's glory (2:11). To accept Jesus is to open oneself up to that transforming experience wherein the Father glorifies the Son in his passion-death-exaltation. That glory is the basis for the Christian's eternal life. Once again Jesus functions as the Revealer and Revelation of God.

Jesus Speaks about His Hour (12:20-33)

John links the arrival of the first Gentiles ('Greeks') to Jesus' statement about the arrival of his 'hour'. Here 'hour' sums up the salvific process of death, resurrection, and ascension. In the face of such universalism Jesus is ready to lay down his life. In verses 23, 27-28 John has his version of Jesus' agony in the garden: (1) hour (Mark 14:41); (2) expression of grief (Mark 14:34); (3) prayer (Mark 14:35-36); and (4) perhaps an angel (Luke 22:43).

Verses 24-26 are the Johannine Jesus' view of life and death. In the parable of the seed (v 24) Jesus explains that his death will effect life for all (see v 32) – more specifically, that only death brings life. Verse 25 ('love/lose, hate/preserve') indicates that like the master, the disciple must embrace death to gain eternal life (see Mark 8:35). In verse 26 to serve Jesus is to follow him (see Mark 8:34) and be honored by the Father. 'Eternal life' (v 25) is bound up with being related to Jesus in the Father's love.

The Jesus of John also experiences great fear in the face of suffering and death. He is thus tempted to abandon the Father's plan. Yet he prays that this plan be executed (v 28: 'Father, glorify your name'). To reassure Jesus, the Father speaks from heaven. The past glorification (v 28: 'I have glorified') may include not only the past ministry but also the 'hour'. The future glorification (v 28: 'will glorify it again') would then look to Jesus' exaltation with the Father (see 13:31-32). In verse 31 Jesus' 'hour' brings about the loss of Satan's authority ('the ruler of this world'). Against the background of the Suffering Servant in Isaiah 52:13, Jesus' being lifted up means his exaltation, indeed one preceded by death that results in a new relationship for all people (v 32: 'I will draw everyone to myself' – see Jeremiah 31:3). Verse 33 is an editorial insertion explaining that his being lifted up means his crucifixion (see 18:31-32).

The Book of Glory and the First Conclusion of the Gospel (13:1 – 20:31)

Jesus Washes the Disciples' Feet (13:1-15)

Chapters 13 to 17 of John are Jesus' farewell discourses. In such a discourse a speaker announces his imminent departure and recalls past events, words, etc., so that the addressees can imitate them or even surpass them. In effect, the discourse looks more to the future than the past (see Moses in Deuteronomy 33 and Joshua in Joshua 23-24). John provides the introduction to the farewell discourses in 13:31-38.

Verse 1, the beginning of the Book of Glory, understands Jesus' death under two aspects: (1) an act of love for his followers; and (2) victory because of Jesus' return to the Father. In verse 2 John links the footwashing to Jesus' death by noting the betrayal of Judas and, in verse 3, by stressing Jesus' return to the Father. The footwashing itself (vv 4-5) is an act of humility on Jesus' part, *i.e.*, he plays the role of a servant, a role symbolic of his humiliation in death.

Verses 6-10a are the first and more original interpretation of the symbolic action. The footwashing renders the disciple capable of enjoying eternal life (v 8: ' have inheritance with me') with Jesus. Verses 9-10a develop this in terms of a baptismal interpretation ('bathe'), *i.e.*, sharing in Jesus' death cleanses one from sin. Verses 10b-11 are an editorial insertion, indicating that the footwashing had not produced any change in Judas.

Verses 12-15 are part of the second interpretation. The footwashing demonstrates Jesus' service on behalf of others – a quality that his followers must imitate. If the teacher and master deigned to wash the feet of his disciples, then the disciples must be willing to wash one another's feet. John 15:12-13 will interpret this self-giving to include even laying down one's life.

Jesus Gives the New Commandment of Mutual Love (13:31-33a,34-35)

This passage introduces Jesus' farewell discourses. The 'now' (v 31) refers to the departure of Judas that provokes Jesus' passage from this world. In verses 31-35 John has combined three themes: (1) Jesus' glorification (vv 31-32); (2) his departure (v 33); and (3) the commandment of mutual love (vv 34-35). Although Jesus must leave the disciples, obedience to his commandment ensures his abiding presence.

Jesus' glorification is the entire process running from the passion to the ascension (v 31). This finally leads to the glory that Jesus will enjoy in the Father's presence (v 32). 'My children' (v 33) is a term of affection that suits the farewell discourse strategy in which a father or leader takes leave of his family or community. The commandment of mutual love resolves the problem of Jesus' departure. This is a love among believers that finds its source in the self-giving love of Jesus. Wherever such love is found, outsiders will recognize them as disciples of Jesus.

The newness of this love derives from the Father's giving of the Son.

This newness also flows from the new covenant or new relationship that is part of the Last Supper scene (see Jeremiah 31:31-34; Luke 22:20). This meal symbolizes the Christian acceptance of the commandment of mutual love. (Unlike the Synoptics, John situates the Eucharist in chapter 6, not at the Last Supper.)

Jesus Describes Himself as the Way, the Truth and the Life (14:1-12)

This passage may be outlined as follows: (1) Jesus' departure and return (vv 1-4); (2) misunderstanding about 'way' (v 5); (3) Jesus as the way (vv 6-11); and (4) believing in Jesus (v 12 with vv 13-14).

This farewell discourse is caught up in an atmosphere of Jesus' imminent departure. The 'troubled hearts' (v 1) describe the subsequent battle between the forces of evil ('the world') and the disciples of Jesus upon the latter's departure. Originally verses 1-3 dealt with Jesus' return after death, when he would take the disciples to heaven (v 2: 'my Father's house'). However, it was later reinterpreted to focus attention on the union between the disciple and Jesus/God. 'My Father's house' is thus the body of Jesus (see 2:19-22; 8:35).

As the way, Jesus is the unique means of salvation. As the truth, he is the revelation of the Father. As the life, he is the communication of the life he shares with the Father (see Psalm 86:11; Proverbs 5:6). Verses 7-11 then develop the implications of verse 6. To know Jesus, *i.e.*, to acknowledge Jesus, is to know and acknowledge the Father (v 7). To see Jesus is to see the Father (v 9). After the manner of Deuteronomy 18:18, Jesus is the emissary of the Father. His words and deeds point beyond, namely, to the intimate bond between the Father and himself (v 10). Finally, in verse 12 John connects faith to the present task of the believer. To believe in Jesus is to be empowered to perform the works of Jesus. To be united with Jesus and the Father is to share their power.

Jesus Links His Abiding Presence with the Role of the Advocate/Paraclete (14:15-21)

In the ancient Near East and in the Old Testament 'to love' can also mean 'to obey'. In Deuteronomy 6:5 Israel is to love the Lord by keeping the terms of the covenant relationship. In Johannine theology commandments are not mere moral prescriptions. Rather, they embody a whole way of life, namely, union with Jesus. Verse 21 restates verse 15 and shows that love and the keeping of the commandments are two dimensions of the same way of life (see Wisdom 6:12,18).

In verses 15-17 and 18-21 the keeping of Jesus' commandments is linked to the promise of divine presence. In verses 16-17 the Spirit ('another Advocate/Paraclete') will complement the work of Jesus (the first Advocate/Paraclete during his earthly mission – see 1 John 2:1). The Advocate/Paraclete will not only be with the disciples (v 16); he will also be within them (v 17). Even though the farewell discourses emphasize the departure of Jesus, the Advocate/Paraclete stresses the ongoing presence of Jesus.

In verses 18-21 it is Jesus who will come to dwell with the disciples (note the presence of Jesus and the Father in verses 23-24). The disciples will not be orphaned by the departure of Jesus. Instead, Jesus will continue to abide with his community in the time after his resurrection, for they will share the life of Jesus who shares it with the Father. The eventual uniting described in verses 15-17 and 18-21 informs the reader that Jesus' presence is brought about in and through the Advocate/Paaclete. We thus have one and the same presence.

Jesus Assures His Disciples that the Advocate/Paraclete Will Develop His Teaching (14:23-29)

Against the background of the farewell discourses the command not to fear (v 27) and the insistence on the greeting 'peace' (v 27) have greater urgency. This passage consists of the following three sections: (1) the coming of the Father to the believer (vv 23-24); (2) the mission of the Advocate/Paraclete to teach (vv 25-26); and (3) the gift of peace and Jesus' departure (vv 27-29).

'Word' is synonymous with words or commandments. Whoever refuses to keep Jesus' covenantal demands is divorced from that life that only Jesus can bring. On the contrary, whoever keeps Jesus' covenantal demands will enjoy that life, namely, the indwelling of the Father and Jesus.

How is the Christian community to function after Jesus' departure? A key concept here is the role of the Advocate/Paraclete. Actually Jesus is the first Advocate/Paraclete. The Holy Spirit is 'another Advocate/Paraclete' (14:16) whom the Father will send in Jesus' name. One function of the Advocate/Paraclete is to develop the teaching of Jesus. 'To remind' (v 26) is not to recall an event statically but to live the implications of Jesus' word at a later date.

At the moment the attitude of the disciples is possessiveness. They are not yet ready to let Jesus depart and so complete his mission. The disciples cannot love because they do not believe. Once they come to accept in faith the mission of Jesus and thus his need to depart, they will be able to love Jesus. To frustrate the Father's plan is to refuse to love.

Jesus Presents the Parable of the Vine and the Branches (15:1-8)

This passage is a parable that contains certain allegorical elements (*e.g.*, Jesus = the vine, the Father = the vinegrower). John 15:7-17 then adapts and develops this imagery within the framework of the farewell discourses.

The Old Testament frequently uses the vine as a symbol for God's people, Israel (Ezekiel 15:1-6; 17:5-10; Hosea 10:1). Here John applies the imagery to Jesus but in such a way that the new Israel, the branches, are part of the vine. Jesus claims to be the real vine, *i.e.*, the one who brings genuine life from the Father. There may also be a reference to the false vine, namely, the Israel whom God has rejected for being unfruitful (see Isaiah 5:1-7; Mark 12:1-12). Not to bear fruit is not to share in that genuine life/vine and hence to be dead. But to share in that life/vine is to share it with others (v 2: 'bear more fruit'). In verse 3, perhaps inserted into the parable in its new setting, Jesus' word in this farewell discourse prunes the disciples. But the pruning implies response, *i.e.*, remaining in Jesus (v 4). Productivity is bound up with this intimate, personal union. To be apart from Jesus means to be unproductive (v 5) and to be unproductive means to suffer final punishment (see Matthew 3:10).

In verse 7 John applies the parable to the farewell discourse setting. Union with Jesus means a life founded on Jesus' words or revelation. Harmony with that revelation means the fulfillment of any and all requests. Verse 8 shows that these requests look to productivity and discipleship. The Father, the vinegrower, is glorified in the disciples who continue the mission of the Son (12:28).

Jesus Applies the Parable of the Vine and the Branches by Stressing the Role of Mutual Love (15:9-17)

This passage adapts and develops the imagery of the parable about the vine and the branches (15:1-6) within the framework of the farewell discourse. In verse 9 John introduces the theme of love that is linked to remaining in Jesus' love that, in turn, has its origin in the Father's love. 'To remain in' means to acknowledge Jesus' love by responding and, indeed, by responding to Jesus' commandments. The union of the disciple with Jesus will effect joy, a joy that Jesus first experienced by fidelity to the Father (14:31).

Jesus now informs the disciples that the fundamental commandment is love. Mutual love flows from Jesus' love of the disciples that flows from the Father's love of Jesus. Jesus' death for others is the specific model that John holds up for his audience. Such a love constitutes the circle of Jesus' intimates. These intimates are made privy to the word that Jesus has received from the Father. Jesus chose the disciples, not *vice versa*. However, their election envisions going on mission for others (v 16: 'go and bear fruit'). Enduring productivity assures the disciples that the Father will heed their requests. 'Love one another ' (v 17) is the appropriate conclusion of this section.

Jesus Emphasizes the Role of the Advocate/Paraclete as Teacher (16:12-15)

This passage focuses on this question: How will one preserve and really understand the message of Jesus? John addresses this question by developing the role of the Advocate/Paraclete as the teacher of the disciples. What is at stake is a deeper penetration of the mystery of Jesus. The Advocate/Paraclete functions here after the manner of Lady Wisdom. He guides the disciples along the way of truth. As in Proverbs, it is a question of life, namely, a life in keeping with Jesus' teaching.

'Declaring the things that are coming' (v 13) looks to the significance of Jesus for each new generation. One cannot simply ask: 'What did Jesus teach?' Rather, one must ask: 'What does that teaching mean for me today?' As guide and teacher, the Advocate/Paraclete resolves this problem of the generation gap.

John also develops the roles of the Father, Jesus, and the Advocate/Paraclete. As the Revealer and Revelation of God, Jesus glorifies the Father (17:4). By revealing Jesus, the Advocate/Paraclete glorifies Jesus. The Advocate/Paraclete, moreover, announces not only the Son but also the Father since Father and Son possess everything in common.

Jesus Prays to the Father on His Own Behalf and on Behalf of His Disciples and All Believers (17:1-11a)

In a farewell discourse the speaker often concludes with a prayer for those left behind. For example, in Deuteronomy 32:1 Moses appeals to the heavens but then invokes a blessing on the tribes for the future at the start of his farewell discourse (Deuteronomy 33:1). Although Jesus addresses the Father in this passage, the burden of the prayer touches the disciples. Even if Jesus' exaltation has not yet taken place, one senses that Jesus has already ascended to the Father and that the disciples are privy to a private exchange. The intimacy of this exchange is heightened by the frequent use of the title 'Father' (vv 1,5,11,21,24,25). While the glory and divinity of Jesus figure significantly in this prayer, Jesus' dependence on the Father is also marked.

Chapter 17 may be divided as follows: (1) Jesus' prayer for his own glorification (vv 1-8); (2) his prayer for the disciples (vv 9-19); and (3) his prayer for all those who will eventually believe (vv 20-26). 'Glory' (v 1) connotes the external manifestation of majesty by acts of power. The 'glory', *e.g.*, at Cana (2:11), was a sign that would only be fully realized at the hour of Jesus' exaltation. Jesus will glorify the Father by giving eternal life that, in turn, will beget new disciples. Significantly, Jesus does not pursue his own good on his return to the Father but the good of the disciples. Verses 4-5 reveal Jesus' petition for glory on the basis of what he has already accomplished. Like Lady Wisdom (see Proverbs 8:23,30; Wisdom 7:25), Jesus requests the glory he shared prior to creation itself. In verse 6 the work that glorified the Father was the communication of God's name ('I am') to the disciples. As a result of that revelation, the disciples are aware that everything Jesus has – his message – comes from the Father.

In verse 9 Jesus directly includes the disciples in his prayer. It will be through their efforts that God's name, confided to Jesus, will be glorified. Indeed, Jesus has already been glorified in them. The 'world' expresses the totality of forces opposed to Jesus' revelation of the Father. In this gospel the 'world' must cease to be 'world' in order to be saved.

Jesus Prays for the Consecration of the Disciples (17:11b-19)

In this part of Jesus' prayer the situation of the disciples is paramount. They do not belong to the 'world' (vv 14,16). Yet Jesus gives them his Father's word and sends them into the 'world' (v 18) to provoke faith in him. Yet the 'world' responds with hatred (v 14). Jesus, therefore, prays that the Father protect them with his divine name (see Proverbs 18:10). In the midst of pain and frustration they will nonetheless experience great joy (v 13). By sharing the mission of Jesus, they also share the joy of Jesus.

In verses 17-19 John deals with the consecration of Jesus and the disciples. The disciples are to be holy because of their mission. Specifically, they are consecrated in the truth, namely, God's word. That word has purified them (15:3) and sends them forth to provoke faith (20). With regard to Jesus' self-consecration John may have in mind Jesus' voluntary sacrifice of his life (10:17-18; see Hebrews 9:12-14). Jesus' self-consecration in death sanctifies the disciples for their mission.

Jesus Prays for the Unity of All Believers (17:20-26)

This passage concludes both Jesus' prayer and the farewell discourses. Verses 20-23 deal with the unity of those who believe in Jesus, while verses 24-26 are Jesus' wish that such believers be with him. The prayer of Jesus is admittedly a fitting finale for the farewell discourses.

In verses 20-23 the unity of believers that is modeled on the unity between the Father and Jesus will challenge the 'world' to accept Jesus' mission (v 21: 'that you sent me'). This unity of believers is two-dimensional. First of all, it reflects the unity between the Father and the Son. Secondly, it makes the believers into a community. A community that lacks unity among its members can hardly reflect the unity between the Father and Jesus.

In verses 24-26 Jesus' final wish is that believers should share his company. There is, consequently, a final revelation reserved for these believers in heaven. Indeed it is appropriate that these believers should be finally united to Jesus since they have been his intimates on earth. Verse 26 identifies the Father's love for Jesus with the presence of Jesus himself. Such a presence is clearly dynamic.

John Narrates the Passion and Death of Jesus as the Moment of His Glorification (18:1–19:42)

Through his passion account John announces that Jesus' death is an act of complete self-giving and constitutes the final revelation of God's saving love for the world. This account of Jesus' death culminates his mission from the Father and in this 'hour' returns him triumphantly to the Father. From his position on the cross Jesus stands in judgment over the enormous powers of darkness and death and at the same time passes judgment on all other manifestations of power.

This account consists of three parts: (1) Jesus' arrest and questioning (18:1-27); (2) his trial before Pilate (18:28–19:16a); and (3) his crucifixion, death, and burial (19:16b-42). In a sense the word 'passion' is not totally accurate since the pain of Jesus' experience is subsumed under his royalty. Thus John places the agony in the garden in 12:27-28, outside the passion narrative. The soldiers crown him and mock him (19:2-3) because Pilate has proclaimed him a king (18:37). The *Ecce Homo* scene (19:5) is another element in the coronation ritual, namely, the acclamation of the people. Finally, the crucifixion itself is the actual enthronement because his kingship is now announced to the international community (see the trilingual inscription in 19:19-20).

John also emphasizes the absolute freedom of Jesus. He is completely self-possessed, the master of his own fate. Thus only in John does Jesus reply to the indignities before the Jewish officials (18:21). In his 'lecture' to Pilate (19:9-11) he implies that no one takes his life away; rather, he lays it down freely (see 10:18). Unlike the Synoptics, John has no Simon of Cyrene to help Jesus carry his cross. Jesus freely accepts his destiny alone (19:17).

Two other noteworthy departures from the Synoptics are: (1) the presence/function of Jesus' mother and the Beloved Disciple (19:25-27); and (2) the flow of blood and water (19:34). In the first scene Jesus provides for the community he leaves behind. Mary, Lady/Mother Zion (see Isaiah 54:1; 66:7-11), becomes the mother of the Beloved Disciple, the model disciple. She will care for that community and, in turn, the community will respond in terms of mutual love. In the second scene the flow of water is linked to Jesus' own prophecy that from within him there would flow rivers of living water (7:37-38). John relates this to Jesus' deliverance of his spirit (19:30). Jesus' death is antecedently that glorification that will release the Spirit upon the new community (see 7:39; 20:22).

Jesus Acknowledges His Kingship before Pilate (18:33b-37)

In this passage kingship plays a dominant role. Involvement is also a key issue. Pilate does not want to get involved with God's word. He wishes to avoid the task of judging and so vacillates when Jesus questions him about the title 'the King of the Jews'. This, in turn, provokes the discussion of handing Jesus over. Jesus replies that his kingship is different. It is non-political and non-national. It is one of truth, *i.e.*, one concerned with the revelation of God's word. Ironically, Jesus is on trial, yet he is the judge whose word provokes a decision. Jesus thus provokes the vacillating Pilate to make a decision and take a stand on the side of truth. But Pilate is not committed to the truth and hence cannot hear God's voice.

John Narrates the Visits of Mary Magdalene, Peter and the Beloved Disciple to the Tomb (20:1-9)

John's account of the empty tomb consists of two parts: (1) Mary of Magdala's arrival and subsequent report (vv 1-2); and (2) the arrival of Simon Peter and the Beloved Disciple, whose reactions differ markedly (vv 3-10). These accounts have different layers. The first originally spoke of the women, not just Mary of Magdala (note 'we' in v 2). The second originally spoke of Simon Peter and an unnamed disciple who was later changed to the Beloved Disciple (contrast v 8, where the Beloved Disciple believes, with v 9 where 'they did not yet understand').

For John, the Beloved Disciple explains the meaning of the empty tomb. The burial cloths pointed to the resurrection of Jesus: 'he saw and believed' (v 8). In contrast to Simon Peter, the Beloved Disciple comes to faith. For John, therefore, the Beloved Disciple becomes the model to be followed. His love for Jesus has led him to believe the mystery of Jesus. Death could not be the Father's final gesture.

The Risen Jesus Appears to the Disciples (minus Thomas) on Easter Sunday Evening (20:19-23)

John collapses the resurrection/ascension/Pentecost into the happenings of Easter Sunday (see vv 17,19). 'Peace' (v 19) is not a simple greeting. It conjures up the divine presence (see Judges 6:24) that will become permanent in the bestowal of the Spirit. The emphasis on the wounds suggests the continuity between the crucifixion and the resurrection. The disciples' reaction is one of faith (v 20: 'the Lord'). In verse 21 Jesus makes his relationship with the Father the model for the disciples' mission. They will thus continue Jesus' mission by offering life to all believers (6:39-40). Breathing (v 22) symbolizes a new creation (see Genesis 2:7). Moreover, the presence of the Spirit resolves the problem of the absence of Jesus. For John, 'sin' (v 23) has a special meaning: the refusal to believe in Jesus. The disciples will exercise their mission by forgiving/retaining sins, forcing people to judge themselves. John does not mention how that power will be exercised. He speaks of the disciples, not the Eleven. One should note that all the disciples come under God's new creation in verse 22.

The Risen Jesus Appears a Week later to to His Disciples (including Thomas) (20:19-31)

This passage consists of two episodes and a conclusion. The first episode (vv 19-23) deals with Jesus' appearance to the disciples (for which see above). The second episode (vv 24-29) deals with Jesus' appearance to Thomas. Probably the latter appearance is an expansion of the former. The disciples' doubt in 20:20 is thus magnified in Thomas who serves the needs of John's community. Finally, the author's conclusion (vv 30-31) applies the challenge of faith to future generations.

In the Thomas episode John speaks to those believers who never knew and never would know the historical Jesus. Those who knew him and believed are not put down. However, a new type of faith is called for in the post-apostolic period, a faith without benefit of eyewitnesses. 'My Lord and my God!' (v 28) echoes the reply of the new covenant people who will accept Jesus. This attitude is prolonged in the conclusion. After stating the purpose of his work, John challenges his community to look beyond the signs and come to faith in Jesus.

Epilogue
(21:1-25)

The Risen Jesus Appears to Seven Disciples in Galilee and Rehabilitates and Commissions Peter (21:1-19)

This passage is an epilogue, the work of a redactor who wanted to preserve certain traditions for the Johannine community. The resurrection appearances here are autonomous and reflect a Galilean tradition that is independent of the Jerusalem traditions found in chapter 20. As it now stands, this passage consists of the following: (1) the appearance of the risen Jesus to the disciples at the Sea of Tiberias (a fishing scene [vv 1-8], a meal on land [vv 9-13], and an observation [v 14]); and (2) Simon Peter's rehabilitation and fate (vv 15-19).

The catch of fish and the meal on land were originally two different accounts. In the first Jesus appears to be without fish (v 5), yet when the disciples arrive, he has already prepared a fish (v 9). Simon Peter and the Beloved Disciple recognize Jesus because of the large catch (v 7), but later there is some dispute about Jesus' identity (v 12). It is possible that we are dealing here with Jesus' appearance to Peter (1 Corinthians 15:5) and then on another occasion to the other disciples. Thus, after the crucifixion Peter returned to Galilee and resumed his old profession. At the lake Peter saw Jesus and recognized him (see Matthew 14:28). 'Depart from me, Lord, for I am a sinful man' (Luke 5:8) probably belongs here. Jesus, however, not only forgives Peter but also confers a leadership position on him in his Church. It is also likely that Jesus appeared to the other disciples at a meal of bread and fish (see Luke 24:30-31).

In this joint account (vv 1-13) there is ample symbolism. The catch of fish is no longer the disciples' clue to Jesus' identity. It symbolizes their apostolic mission, for they are now fishers of human beings (Luke 5:10). Jesus' action at the meal points to the Eucharist: ' ... took the bread and gave it to them and in like manner the fish' (v 13). This scene is reminiscent of Jesus' action at the multiplication of loaves and fish (6:11). For the reader, this establishes a link between the Eucharist and the presence of the risen Lord in the community.

The dramatic dialogue between Jesus and Peter (vv 15-17) is the Johannine form of Peter's rehabilitation and commission. It consists of a threefold question by Jesus, a threefold answer by Peter, and a threefold response by Jesus. The thrust of Jesus' threefold question and Peter's threefold answer is to demonstrate that Peter's love for Jesus is genuine. Jesus' threefold response (feeding lambs/sheep, tending sheep) is perhaps a borrowing from the ancient Near Eastern custom of emphasizing by repetition, *i.e.*, the statement is authoritative. In the Old Testament, pasturing the flock (Ezekiel 34:2) and shepherding the flock (Ezekiel 34:10) are the tasks of kings. (The Greek verb translated 'to tend' [v 16] has the connotation of ruling and governing [see 2 Samuel 7:7].) Jesus, the model shepherd (10:11), gives Peter responsibility for the flock and authority over it.

Verses 18-19 are probably an independent unit added to link Peter's future with his death. Verse 18 contrasts Peter as a young man and as an older man. As an older man, he will follow Jesus in suffering (see the binding of Jesus in 18:12,24). Verse 19 makes explicit the precise form of suffering, namely, death by crucifixion (12:33; 18:32). The command to follow entails following Jesus both in discipleship and in death.

Concluding Reflections on the Jesus of John

Compared to the Synoptics, John presents a more exalted and a more theologically profound Jesus. As noted earlier, the Jesus of John is the Revealer and Revelation of God. He has left his unique place in the company of the Father to pitch his tent (1:14) among humans in order to communicate who his Father is and what he demands from them. According to the prologue the Jesus of John is nothing less than the word of God. Like Lady Wisdom in the Old Testament, he invites people to enjoy genuine life by provoking them to take a stand on the issue of this life. Emulating Lady Wisdom, the Jesus of John announces: 'Forsake foolishness that you may live; advance in the way of understanding' (Proverbs 9:6).

The Jesus of John challenges his audience to judge reality from God's perspective. To achieve this, John often uses the device of misunderstanding. Thus Jesus will use metaphors or figurative language to develop his message. His dialogue partner will then misunderstand Jesus' expressions. In turn, this misunderstanding permits Jesus to pursue his message in greater depth. For example, the Samaritan woman misunderstands the meaning of Jesus' 'living water' (4:10) by thinking of ordinary water from a well. This then permits Jesus to explain that 'living water' is actually the revelation he brings from his Father (4:14). In this same chapter Jesus' disciples urge him to eat (4:31). Jesus responds to their request by speaking of food of which they are unaware (4:32). This leads the disciples to think only on the level of bodily nourishment (4:33). This misunderstanding presents the opportunity to teach that his food is really the accomplishment of his mission from the Father (4:34).

The Jesus of John also performs miracles but, as opposed to the Synoptics, they are intended to be signs, *i.e.*, indications of who Jesus is and what his message really is. While the Jesus of John performs only seven such signs, they serve as important clues as to his identity and revelatory message. As seen in the multiplication of loaves and fish, the Jesus of John is the Bread of Life (6:34). He is the one who supplies what is contained in the religious symbol of bread. As bread maintains life, Jesus will also maintain life in all those who come to him. As the Bread of Life, Jesus is not only the Revealer and Revelation of the Father but also the source of that nourishment that leads to eternal life (6:54). In the healing of the man born blind, the Jesus of John is the Light of the World (9:5). As such, he triumphs over all forms of darkness by sharing his message with all those who come to him to seek the light of faith.

The Jesus of John emphasizes the role of the Spirit in unfolding his revelation. Jesus' death, that is not a defeat but a triumph, releases the Spirit to continue his mission. As noted in the farewell discourses, the Spirit is another Advocate/Paraclete (14:16), *i.e.*, Jesus is the first Advocate/Paraclete and the Spirit continues his work in a variety of ways. In this manner the Spirit complements the mission of Jesus by performing these functions: consoling, teaching, guiding, witnessing, defending. By operating in this way, the Spirit, as Advocate/Paraclete, resolves the problem of Jesus' absence.

Liturgical Index

Year A in the Lectionary

Advent, First Sunday (Mt 24:37-44)	57
Advent Second Sunday (Mt 3:1-12)	36
Advent, Third Sunday (Mt 11:2-11)	44
Advent Fourth Sunday (Mt 1:18-24)	34
Christmas, Vigil (Mt 1:1-25)	34
Christmas, Midnight Mass (Lk 2:1-14)	68
Christmas, Dawn Mass (Lk 2:15-20)	69
Christmas, Day Mass (Jn 1:1-18)	104
Holy Family (Mt 2:13-15.19-23)	35
Christmas, Octave (Lk 2:16-21)	70
Second Sunday after Christmas (Jn1:1-18)	104
Epiphany of the Lord (Mt 2:1-12)	35
Baptism of the Lord (m 3:13-17)	37
Lent, First Sunday (Mt 4:1-11)	37
Lent, Second Sunday (Mt 17:1-9)	51
Lent, Third Sunday (Jn 4:5-42)	109
Lent, Fourth Sunday (Jn 9:1-41)	113
Lent, Fifth Sunday (Jn 11:1-45)	115
Palm Sunday (Mt 26:14–27:66)	60
Holy Thursday (Jn 13:1-15)	116
Good Friday (Jn 18:1–19.42)	123
Easter Vigil (Mt 28:1-10)	60
Easter, Easter Sunday (Jn 20:1-9)	124
Easter, Second Sunday (Jn 20:19-31)	125
Easter, Third Sunday (Lk 24:13-35)	98
Easter, Fourth Sunday (Jn 10:1-10).	113
Easter, Fifth Sunday (Jn 14:1-12)	118
Easter, Sixth Sunday (Jn 14:15-21)	118
Ascension (Mt 28:16-20)	61
Easter, Seventh Sunday (Jn 17:1-11)	121
Pentecost, Vigil Mass (Jn 7:37-39)	112
Pentecost, Day Mass (Jn 20:19-23)	125
Trinity Sunday (Jn 3:16-18)	108
Corpus Christi (Jn 51-58)	111
Ordinary Time, Second Sunday (Jn 1:29-34)	106
Ordinary Time, Third Sunday (Mt 4:12-23)	38
Ordinary Time, Fourth Sunday (Mt 5:1-12)	38
Ordinary Time, Fifth Sunday (Mt 5:13-16)	39
Ordinary Time, Sixth Sunday (Mt 5:17-37)	40
Ordinary Time, Seventh Sunday (Mt 5:38-48)	41
Ordinary Time, Eighth Sunday (Mt 6:24-34)	41
Ordinary Time, Ninth Sunday (Mt 7:21-27)	42
Ordinary Time, Tenth Sunday (Mt 9:9-13)	42
Ordinary Time, Eleventh Sunday (Mt 9:36–10:8)	43
Ordinary Time, Twelfth Sunday (Mt 10:26-33)	43
Ordinary Time, Thirteenth Sunday (Mt 10:37-42)	44
Ordinary Time, Fourteenth Sunday (Mt 11:25-30)	45
Ordinary Time, Fifteenth Sunday (Mt 13:1-23)	46
Ordinary Time, Sixteenth Sunday (Mt 13:24-43)	47
Ordinary Time, Seventeenth Sunday (Mt 13:44-52)	47
Ordinary Time, Eighteenth Sunday (Mt 14:13-21)	48

Ordinary Time, Nineteenth Sunday (Mt 14:22-33)	49	Ordinary Time, Twenty-eighth Sunday (Mt 22:1-14)	55
Ordinary Time, Twentieth Sunday (Mt 15:21-28)	49	Ordinary Time, Twenty-ninth Sunday (Mt 22:15-21)	56
Ordinary Time, Twenty-first Sunday (Mt 16:13-20)	50	Ordinary Time, Thirtieth Sunday (Mt 22:34-40)	56
Ordinary Time, Twenty-second Sunday (Mt 16:21-27)	51	Ordinary Time, Thirty-first Sunday (Mt 23:1-12)	57
Ordinary Time, Twenty-third Sunday (Mt 18:15-20)	52	Ordinary Time, Thirty-second Sunday (Mt 25:1-13)	58
Ordinary Time, Twenty-fourth Sunday (Mt 18:21-35)	53	Ordinary Time, Thirty-third Sunday (Mt 25:14-30)	59
Ordinary Time, Twenty-fifth Sunday (Mt 20:1-16)	53	Ordinary Time, Thirty-fourth Sunday Christ the King: (Mt 25:31-46)	59
Ordinary Time, Twenty-sixth Sunday (Mt 21:28-32)	54	Assumption of Mary (Lk 1:39-56)	67
Ordinary Time, Twenty-seventh Sunday (Mt 21:33-43)	54	All Saints (Mt 5:1-11)	38
		Immaculate Conception (Lk 1:26-38)	66

Year B in the Lectionary

Advent, First Sunday (Mk 13:33-37)	27	Easter, Easter Sunday (Jn 20:1-9)	124
Advent, Second Sunday (Mk 1:1-8)	10	Easter, Second Sunday (Jn 20:19-31)	125
Advent, Third Sunday (Jn 1:6-8.19-28)	105	Easter, Third Sunday (Lk 24:35-48)	98
Advent, Fourth Sunday (Lk 1:26-38)	66	Easter, Fourth Sunday (Jn 10:11-18)	114
Christmas, Vigil (Mt 1:1-25)	34	Easter, Fifth Sunday (Jn 15:1-8)	120
Christmas, Midnight Mass (Lk 2:1-14)	68	Easter, Sixth Sunday (Jn 15:9-17)	120
Christmas, Dawn Mass (Lk 2:15-20)	69	Ascension (Mk 16:15-20)	30
Christmas, Day Mass (Jn 1:1-10)	104	Easter, Seventh Sunday (Jn 17:11-19)	122
Holy Family (Lk 2:22-40)	70	Pentecost, Vigil Mass (Jn 7:37-39)	112
Christmas, Octave (Lk 2:16-21)	70	Pentecost, Day Mass (Jn 15:26-27; 16:12-15)	125
Second Sunday after Christmas (Jn 1:1-18)	104	Trinity Sunday (Mt 28:16-20)	61
Epiphany of the Lord (Mt 2:1-12)	35	Corpus Christi (Mk 14:12-16.22-26)	29
Baptism of the Lord (Mk 1:7-11)	10	Ordinary Time, Second Sunday (Jn 1:35-42)	106
Lent, First Sunday (Mk 1:12-15)	11	Ordinary Time, Third Sunday (Mk 1:14-20)	11
Lent, Second Sunday (Mk 9:2-10)	22	Ordinary Time, Fourth Sunday (Mk 1:21-28)	12
Lent, Third Sunday (Jn 2:12-25)	107	Ordinary Time, Fifth Sunday (Mk 1:29-39)	13
Lent, Fourth Sunday (Jn 3:14-21)	108	Ordinary Time, Sixth Sunday (Mk 1:40-45)	13
Lent, Fifth Sunday (Jn 12:20-30)	116		
Palm Sunday (Mk 14:1–15:47)	28		
Holy Thursday (Jn 13:1-15)	116		
Good Friday (Jn 18:1–19:42)	123		
Easter Vigil (Mk 16:1-7)	30		

Liturgical Index: Year C in the Lectionary

Ordinary Time, Seventh Sunday (Mk 2:2-12)	14
Ordinary Time, Eighth Sunday (Mk 2:18-22)	14
Ordinary Time, Ninth Sunday (Mk 2:23–3:6)	15
Ordinary Time, Tenth Sunday (Mk 3:20-35)	16
Ordinary Time, Eleventh Sunday (Mk 4:26-34)	16
Ordinary Time, Twelfth Sunday (Mk 4:35-41)	17
Ordinary Time, Thirteenth Sunday (Mk 5:21-43)	18
Ordinary Time, Fourteenth Sunday (Mk 6:1-6)	19
Ordinary Time, Fifteenth Sunday (Mk 6:7-13)	19
Ordinary Time, Sixteenth Sunday (Mk 6:30-34)	20
Ordinary Time, Seventeenth Sunday (Jn 6:1-15)	109
Ordinary Time, Eighteenth Sunday (Jn 6:24-35)	110
Ordinary Time, Nineteenth Sunday (Jn 6:41-53)	111
Ordinary Time, Twentieth Sunday (Jn 6:51-58)	111
Ordinary Time, Twenty-first Sunday (Jn 6:60-69)	111
Ordinary Time, Twenty-second Sunday (Mk 7:1-8.14-15.21-23)	20
Ordinary Time, Twenty-third Sunday (Mk 7:31-37)	21
Ordinary Time, Twenty-fourth Sunday (Mk 8:27-35)	21
Ordinary Time, Twenty-fifth Sunday (Mk 9:30-37)	23
Ordinary Time, Twenty-sixth Sunday (Mk 9:38-43.45.47-48)	23
Ordinary Time, Twenty-seventh Sunday (Mk 10:2-16)	24
Ordinary Time, Twenty-eighth Sunday (Mk 10:17-30)	24
Ordinary Time, Twenty-ninth Sunday (Mk 10:35-45)	25
Ordinary Time, Thirtieth Sunday (Mk 10:46-52)	25
Ordinary Time, Thirty-first Sunday (Mk 12:28-34)	26
Ordinary Time, Thirty-second Sunday (Mk 12:38-44)	26
Ordinary Time, Thirty-third Sunday (Mk 13:24-32)	27
Ordinary Time, Thirty-fourth Sunday Christ the King (Jn 18:33-37)	124
Assumption of Mary (Lk 1:39-56)	67
All Saints (Mt 5:1-11)	38
Immaculate Conception (Lk 1:26-38)	66

Year C in the Lectionary

Advent, First Sunday (Lk 21:25-28.34-36)	94
Advent, Second Sunday (Lk 3:1-6)	72
Advent Third Sunday (Lk 3:10-18)	72
Advent, Fourth Sunday (Lk 1:39-44)	67
Christmas, Vigil (Mt 1:1-25)	34
Christmas, Midnight Mass (Lk 2:1-14)	68
Christmas, Dawn Mass (Lk 2:15-20)	69
Christmas, Day Mass (Jn 1:1-18)	104
Holy Family (Lk 2:41-52)	71
Christmas, Octave (Lk 2:16-21)	70
Second Sunday after Christmas (Jn1:1-18)	104
Epiphany of the Lord (Mt 2:1-12)	35
Baptism of the Lord (Lk 3:15-16.21-22)	73
Lent, First Sunday (Lk 4:1-13)	74
Lent, Second Sunday (Lk 9:28-36)	81
Lent, Third Sunday (Lk 13:1-9)	86
Lent, Fourth Sunday (Lk 15:1-3.11-32)	88
Lent, Fifth Sunday (Jn 8:1-11)	112
Palm Sunday (Lk 22:14–23:56)	95
Holy Thursday (Jn 13:1-15)	116
Good Friday (Jn 18:1–19:42)	123
Easter Vigil (Lk 24:1-12)	97
Easter, Easter Sunday (Jn 20:1-9)	124
Easter, Second Sunday (Jn 20:19-31)	125

Easter, Third Sunday (Jn 21:1-19)	126	Ordinary Time, Seventeenth Sunday (Lk 11:1-13)	84
Easter, Fourth Sunday (Jn 10:27-30)	114	Ordinary Time, Eighteenth Sunday (Lk 12:13-21)	85
Easter, Fifth Sunday (Jn 13:31-35)	117	Ordinary Time, Nineteenth Sunday (Lk 12:32-48)	85
Easter, Sixth Sunday (Jn 14:23-29)	119	Ordinary Time, Twentieth Sunday (Lk 12:49-53)	86
Ascension (Lk 24:46-53)	99	Ordinary Time, Twenty-first Sunday (Lk 13:22-30)	87
Easter, Seventh Sunday (Jn 17:20-26)	122	Ordinary Time, Twenty-second Sunday (Lk 14:1.7-14)	87
Pentecost, Vigil Mass (Jn 7:37-39)	112	Ordinary Time, Twenty-third Sunday (Lk 14:25-33)	88
Pentecost, Day Mass (Jn 14:15-16.23-26)	125	Ordinary Time, Twenty-fourth Sunday (Lk 15:1-32)	88
Trinity Sunday (Jn 16:12-15)	121	Ordinary Time, Twenty-fifth Sunday (Lk 16:1-13	89
Corpus Christi (Lk 9:11-17)	80	Ordinary Time, Twenty-sixth Sunday (Lk 16:19-31)	90
Ordinary Time, Second Sunday (Jn 2:1-11)	107	Ordinary Time, Twenty-seventh Sunday (Lk 17:5-10)	90
Ordinary Time, Third Sunday (Lk 1:1-4; 4:14-21)	74	Ordinary Time, Twenty-eighth Sunday (Lk 17:11-19)	91
Ordinary Time, Fourth Sunday (Lk 4:21-30)	75	Ordinary Time, Twenty-ninth Sunday (Lk 18:1-8)	91
Ordinary Time, Fifth Sunday (Lk 5:1-11)	75	Ordinary Time, Thirtieth Sunday (Lk 18:9-14)	92
Ordinary Time, Sixth Sunday (Lk 6:17.20-26)	76	Ordinary Time, Thirty-first Sunday (Lk 19:1-10)	92
Ordinary Time, Seventh Sunday (Lk 6:27-38)	77	Ordinary Time, Thirty-second Sunday (Lk 20:27-38)	93
Ordinary Time, Eighth Sunday (Lk 6:39-45)	77	Ordinary Time, Thirty-third Sunday (Lk 21:5-19)	94
Ordinary Time, Ninth Sunday (Lk 7:1-10)	78	Ordinary Time, Thirty-fourth Sunday Christ the King (Lk 23:35-43)	96
Ordinary Time, Tenth Sunday (Lk 7:11-17)	78	Assumption of Mary (Lk 1:39-56)	67
Ordinary Time, Eleventh Sunday (Lk 7:36–8:3)	79	All Saints (Mt 5:1-11)	38
Ordinary Time, Twelfth Sunday (Lk 9:18-24)	80	Immaculate Conception (Lk 1:26-38)	66
Ordinary Time, Thirteenth Sunday (Lk 9:51-64)	82		
Ordinary Time, Fourteenth Sunday (Lk 10:1-12.17-20)	82		
Ordinary Time, Fifteenth Sunday (Lk 10:25-37)	83		
Ordinary Time, Sixteenth Sunday (Lk Lk 10:38-42)	84